Be an Explorer. Not a Tourist.

...and Travel With Integrity.

It feels good to support the people and places in this book.
We are about to introduce you to good people,
good places and good businesses that deserve your time.

STOCK OUR BOOK

Want to stock our book in your shop, store, or platform? Send us a message at hello@thesologirlstravelguide.com

the SOLO GIRL'S TRAVEL GUIDE

THAILAND

ALEXA WEST GUIDES

EVERY GIRL SHOULD TRAVEL SOLO
AT LEAST ONCE IN HER LIFE

You don't need a boyfriend, a travel partner or anyone's approval to travel the world. And you don't need a massive bank account or an entire summer off work.

All you need is that wanderlust in your blood and a good guidebook in your hands.

If you've doubted yourself for one moment, remember this:

Millions of girls travel across the globe all by themselves every damn day and you can, too.

You are just as capable, just as smart, and just as brave as the rest of us. You don't need permission – this is your life.

Listen to your gut, follow your heart and remember that the best adventures start with the simple decision to go.

What travelers are saying...

"First of all, let me say that I am still in Thailand as I write this and it will be almost a month soon. Without this book I would've been lost and probably ended my trip sooner. Every recommendation Alexa makes is because she's been there and done that and can tell you first hand! There's no filler and no overly touristy spots like you would get with other guides like Lonely Planet etc etc. she gets straight to the point of telling you what's awesome and what's not."

- Larissa

"I had originally purchased the Lonely Planet travel guide which only overwhelmed me and I was unable to decide what parts of Thailand to go to. This guide narrowed things down for me and allowed me to plan a great trip instead of trying to squeeze too many destinations in. I love the entertaining writing style and quick, to the point suggestions. Will be purchasing your other guides for my future travels!"

- Brittany

"Loved the book! Definitely the ONLY book you will need for the trip (unless you also want to buy the Thailand Islands & Beaches book). This was an absolute must for an amazing week in Thailand with my 2 girlfriends. Great tips and suggestions. Every place we tried from the book was an absolute home run. I don't think the trip would have been as flawlessly great if it were not for the book."

- Sara

Nice to meet you!
I'm Lexi...

I'm not here to get rich or reach 1 million followers on Instagram.
I'm here because I want to change the way we travel as women.

I want to help you find yourself.

I want to fling you to the other side of the world, out of your comfort zone
(but still safe, I got you), and help you get so totally lost that you find yourself.

And I do that by connecting you to the most beautiful places, the kindest
people, the most challenging opportunities, and the most rewarding
experiences.

Do you know what kind of woman this will create?

A happy woman who shines so bright that everyone she comes in contact
with is illuminated too.

I'm here to turn your light up, girl.

I'm here to help you connect to the experiences that will change you. ...and
get the best Instagram photos, too, of course.

To glow up on your travels, remember Travel Karma is real and beautiful.

Travel to give and you will get.

A LITTLE ABOUT ME

Back in 2010, I was a broke-ass Seattle girl who had just graduated from college and had about $200 to my name. I was faced with two choices: get a job, a husband, and have 3 babies plus a mortgage…or sell everything I owned, travel the world and disappoint my parents.

Obviously, I made the right choice.

For the past 10 years, I've been traveling the world solo. I've played every travel role from being the young volunteer and broke backpacker to flying to exotic islands to review new luxury hotels and give breath to struggling tourism industries.

Now I spend my days as an explorer on a mission to change the way that women travel the world. I want to show you places you've never seen and unlock hidden doors you never knew existed in places you may have been before. I want to create a path for you where you feel safe while diving deeper into cultures and countries beyond your own – whether for a week, a year, or a lifetime. And that's what I'm doing.

xoxo, Alexa West

Flights, airports, walking around town…
Travel is a little bit more magical when good music is involved.
Find my thailand playlist here.

ALEXA'S #1 TIP FOR MAKING FRIENDS AS A SOLO TRAVELER

Put your damn phone down.

You didn't come all the way here just to scroll on Instagram, now did you?

People are less likely to approach you when you look so busy on your phone. You have no shot of making eye contact with a stranger if you're staring at reading internet gossip. You miss every opportunity that you do not see.

The next time you're sitting at a bar or on the beach and you have nothing to entertain you, resist the urge to pick up your phone. Resist the addiction. Instead, journal while taking time to look around. Listen to music with one headphone in. Or just sit and watch people walking by.

Hell, next time you need directions, put the phone down. Ask a human. Give yourself every chance to make human contact and watch your world spin into beautiful circumstances you never could have planned.

WANT MORE TRAVEL TIPS?

Join Alexa's travel tip email series. This will change how you travel forever.

Go to TheSoloGirlsTravelGuide.com and sign-up for her newsletter.

Don't forget your map!

To keep the price of this book affordable for you, there are no fancy detailed maps inside.

I've got something even better.

SCAN THE CODE below to get your interactive **THAILAND MAP** that you can travel with on the AREA.

TABLE OF CONTENTS

SEE A GIRL TRAVELING WITH THIS GEAR?

SAY HI.

SHE'S YOUR SISTER IN THE

Solo Girl's Travel Club

CARRY THIS GEAR
AS AN INVITATION TO FRIENDSHIP

COLLECT YOUR GEAR HERE:

OR AT THESOLOGIRLSTRAVELGUIDE.COM

INTRODUCTION TO
Thailand

WELCOME TO THAILAND

Come for the beaches and stay for the food: Thailand is about to blow your mind.

While this tropical paradise is only slightly larger than the state of California, it hosts an impressive geographical diversity with jungles, beaches, tiny Thai villages and cities for you to explore. You could come to Thailand over and over and do something new every time. No two Thailand trips are the same…if you plan them right.

And anyone who ever says they've "done" Thailand clearly doesn't know how to travel Thailand like a pro…but you do (or will, by the end of this book).

The first method of approach? Fly into the sprawling capital city of Bangkok where old culture meets new. Spend the day sightseeing at the Royal Grand

Palace and unwind in the evening by exploring and eating your way through one of Bangkok's never-ending night markets. Or hit the backpacker street of Khao San Road (the oldest backpacker street in the world) and eat scorpions on a stick or some $1 pad Thai while mingling with travelers from all around the world. Or go totally off the beaten path on a DIY street food tour and see where the day takes you (one of my favorite things to do).

After Bangkok, head north towards Chiang Mai where you'll encounter a region covered in jungle terrain home to elephants, waterfalls and some of the most iconic Buddhist temples in the region. This is a town where you can walk and wander for days, ducking down little alleyways and stopping into hole-in-the-wall restaurants.

Next, make your way to the southern peninsula where you'll find two coasts lined with warm turquoise water and dotted with white sand islands.

The west coast is home to the incredible Krabi Province which gives you access to the spectacular Railay Beach, the explorer's island of Koh Lanta, and the party island of Koh Phi Phi.

Bounce over to the east coast where you'll find the Surat Thani province which is best known for the islands of Koh Samui, Koh Phangan and Koh Tao (islands which you can easily hop between).

Okay okay okay, I'm going to restrain myself from telling you more (because there is so much more) and I've only just scratched the surface!

Over 30 million tourists come to Thailand each year - many of them solo girl travelers just like you - and it's easy to see why!

Beyond Thailand's tropical appeal, sea turtles, coral reefs, world-renowned food, elephant sanctuaries, and beaches lined with palm trees...Thailand is also pretty damn safe for us girls. Random street crime is rare, public transportation is easily accessible, locals are generally quite friendly and kind, and you're never alone with fellow travelers around every corner.

After you've had enough of Thailand's secret beaches and brightly colored fish (is that even a thing?), you're just a quick plane ride away from other Southeast Asian destinations such as Cambodia, Vietnam, and Indonesia.

Whether you've got a passport full of stamps or you are planning your first trip alone – Thailand is a bucket-list must! Do not leave this planet without exploring Thailand!

I'm so excited for you. Life will never be the same. Let's do this.

♥ Hey! Do you know how many girls live their whole lives and never even leave their own country?

Look at you go! You're special. Don't forget that.

Thailand 101

The Quick Facts

Language: Thai

Population: 70 Million People

Total Area: 198,120 Sq M (Almost The Same Size As Texas)

Currency: Thai Baht

Time Zone: Gmt+7

Religion: Buddhist

The Food

You think you know Thai food? I promise, you don't. Thai food culture is one of the most diverse food cultures in the world that you will only truly begin to understand once you come to Thailand. And even once in Thailand, it will take a lot of eating to get a grasp at just how different and diverse Thai food can be. There's Thai street food, night market food, Thai restaurants, and even convenience store food that all represent Thai food culture…but even then, Thai food greatly varies by region within Thailand! For example, the southern region of Thailand is home to more muslim populations so you might find curries served with naan bread instead of rice. The northern region of Isaan shares cultural commonalities with their neighbor, Laos, and prepares more grilled meats than fish (which makes sense as this area is landlocked). You could order a Masaman Curry in Surat Thani and it is going to be served differently than if you ordered it in Chiang Mai. So, do you have a favorite curry? Order it everywhere and see how it changes based on the region!

PRO TIP! Thai food is the definition of "same same but different" - a phrase you will hear all too often in Thailand.

The Religion

Thailand is Buddhist and beautifully so! Golden temples, monks in bright orange robes, marigold offerings and the sounds of prayer accompanied by ringing bells - Buddhism in Thailand is something to be celebrated no matter which religion you do or don't follow. For Thais, religion is sacred in a variety of ways. For example, Buddhist holidays like Makha Bucha Day, where you are meant to cleanse your mind, are taken so seriously that alcohol is not sold in the country on this day. On the other hand, you'll find Buddhist temples like Doi Kham in Chiang Mai where locals go to pray to win the lottery. Religion has grown and merged with the times in Thailand. It's serene but also playful.

You & The People

Thailand first started seeing tourism from the west in the 1950s, picked up steam in the 1970's and by the late 90's, was the go-to destination for backpackers. That being said, the way you are received in Thailand by Thai people depends largely on how touristy the area is. You might wander into a touristy area where some Thais have worked in the tourism industry for so long that us travelers are all one-in-the-same and they can't really be bothered to put much effort into niceties. You can't blame them. When this happens, however, all you need to do is off the beaten path (even by a couple of blocks away from the tourist streets) where you'll encounter Thai people who are so welcoming and hospitable - so much so, that I've been invited into strangers' homes for lunch, for dinner, to accompany them on voting day or to drive 5 hours into the mountains to visit their friends who have elephants more times than I can count.

In short, some Thai people might see you as just another tourist but others will welcome you in an instant.

The Crime

As we will get into later in the Crime and Safety section of this guide, Thailand is generally very safe. Tourism is very important to this country and so, tourists are not targets for random violent crime...but may be targets for petty crime. Pick pockets and overcharging slightly are the crimes you're most likely to experience. But traveling the country solo, even into far-off towns and islands, is generally very safe compared to the rest of the world. For example, I feel comfortable getting on a minibus and going 6 hours into the middle of the country and then walking to a hostel or hotel solo, without any anxiety about my safety.

However, please do avoid the southern Songkhla region which experiences periodic civil unrest and hostility towards the Thai government. But don't worry, I will steer you clear of that region in this guide.

The Voltage

The voltage in Thailand is 220 volts. Translation: if you're from the US or UK, your curling iron and hair dryer won't work here but your basic electronics will be fine!

For electric outlets, you'll commonly see Type A and Type C sockets like this.

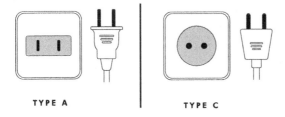

TYPE A | TYPE C

Unless you're carrying sensitive electronics (like said hair dryer) you won't need an international adapter which converts the actual voltage.

You'll just need a plug adapter, like this ☞

☞ **Did You Know?** Thailand has 1,430 islands!?

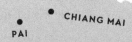

PAI ● ● CHIANG MAI

THAILAND

● UDON THANI

AYUTTHAYA
●

BANGKOK
●

HUA HIN ●

KOH CHANG
ISLANDS

KOH TAO

KOH PHANGAN

KOH SAMUI

KHAO SOK ● ● ········· SURAT THANI

KHAO LAK ········· ●

PHUKET ········· ● KRABI
(+ AO NANG & RAILAY)

KOH PHI PHI

KOH LANTA ········· ●

KOH LIPE

The Mini Thailand Bucket List

TOP 5 THAI TEMPLES

01 Doi Kham, Chiang Mai

02 Doi Suthep, Chiang Mai

03 Wat Phra Yai Temple, Koh Samui

04 Wat Pho (The Emerald Buddha), Bangkok

05 Wat Arun, Bangkok

@IAMCARAAN

TOP 10 THAILAND EXPERIENCES

01 Sleep in Floating Bungalows, Khao Sok National Park

02 Visit an Ethical Elephant Sanctuary in Chiang Mai

03 Take a Cooking Class Anywhere!

04 Krabi Sunset Cruises, Railay Beach

05 Songkran Water Festival, Chiang Mai or Bangkok

06 Srinagarindra Train Night Market, Bangkok

07 Loi Krathong Lantern Festival, Chiang Mai

08 Any food tour in Bangkok

09 Ride in a Longtail Boat Anywhere!

10 Take the Night Train from Bangkok to Chiang Mai or Surat Thani

☞ Check out my blog on the night train here:

TOP 10 THAI BEACHES

01 Railay West, Railay, Krabi

02 Phra Nang Cave Beach, Railay, Krabi

03 W Beach (go to Woo Bar at W Koh Samui), Koh Samui

04 Koh Madsum (Pig Island), Koh Samui

05 There's a Hidden Beach at Treehouse Mae Nam, Koh Samui

06 Bang Por Beach, Koh Samui

07 Bottle Beach, Koh Phangan

08 Nui Beach, *Koh Phi Phi*

09 Monkey Beach, Koh Phi Phi

10 Sairee Beach, Koh Tao

11 Haad Khom, Koh Phangan

TOP 5 THAI MARKETS

---

01 Srinagarindra Train Night Market, *Bangkok*

02 Chatuchak Weekend Market, Bangkok

03 Samrong Fresh Market, Bangkok (the least touristy market in Bangkok)

04 Sunday Market, Chiang Mai

05 Chiang Mai Night Bazaar, Chiang Mai

__Bonus!__

Fisherman's Village Walking Street Friday Night Market, Koh Samui

☞ **WHY NO FLOATING MARKETS ON THIS LIST?**

Well, floating markets have largely become a tourist circus. Many of these markets have fewer and fewer boats in the water and the ones that are there are just selling food for farangs.

At all costs, avoid anyone that tries to sell you a tour to the super touristy Damnoen Saduak Floating Market.

However, there are some floating market experiences that are worth it. Go with Pook on Airbnb experiences (see page 91).

Want super local markets? Explore Samrong or Wang Lang where tourists rarely go.

TOP 10 PLACES TO STAY IN THAILAND

 01 W Hotel, Koh Samui

02 Riviera Beach Hotel, Koh Samui

 03 Avatar Railay, Railay Beach in Krabi

04 Inn a Day, Bangkok

 05 Casa Nithra, Bangkok

06 Bangkok Marriott Hotel Sukhumvit (with Octave Rooftop Bar), Bangkok

 07 Elephant Nature Park, Chiang Mai

08 Floating Bungalows, Khao Sok

 09 Blue Tao Beach Hotel (The Beachfront Room), Koh Tao

10 Baan Boo Loo Village, Chiang Mai

Your Thailand Bucket List

Drink each of the following once...

○ Leo Beer

○ Singha Beer

○ Chang Beer

○ Thai Tea

○ Sangsom Whiskey

Eat each of the following once...

○ Khao Man Gai

○ Penang Curry

○ Larb Gai

○ Khao Soi

○ Khao Ka Moo

○ A 7 Eleven Toastie

Do each of the following once...

○ Get a Thai Massage

○ Order Dinner Speaking in Thai

○ Ride in a Tuk Tuk

○ Eat a Bug

○ Swim in the Ocean

○ Use the GrabTaxi App

○ Ride in a Longtail Boat

○ Sleep in Floating Bungalows

○ Watch the Sunset on the Beach

○ Have Cocktails with a New Friend

THAILAND
Survival Guide

●━━━━━━━━━━━━━●

●━━━━━━━━━━━━━●

COVID Protocol

When it comes to quarantine, vaccines and testing, Thailand is constantly progressing towards finding solutions that make sense for travelers and keep their country safe n' healthy.

To keep you super up to date, I'll keep a blog post that is updated as regulations evolve.

Pro Tip! When searching for hotels on Booking.com, you'll see SHA Plus. This means that at least 70% of staff at the venues and businesses have been fully vaccinated against COVID-19.

Visas for Thailand

Three Options for Tourist Visas for Thailand:

○ **Visa on Arrival via Air**

Fly into Thailand and get a 30 days stamp in your passport—no need to prepare a single document.

○ **Visa on Arrival via Land**

Cross into Thailand by land and get a 30 days stamp in your passport. No need to prepare a single document.

Occasionally, instead of a 30 days visa, Thai immigration will change this tourist allowance to a 15 days visa when crossing over via land. It doesn't happen often, but has happened in the past. Double-check with your Thai embassy's website if you plan to enter Thailand by bus or taxi.

○ 60 days Tourist Visa

Before you come to Thailand, you can go to the nearest Thai Embassy and apply for a 60 days tourist visa. You can do this in any country where there is a Thai Embassy—it doesn't have to be your own country.

It costs about $60 USD & you'll need to have proof of an exit flight. Don't have an exit flight? Check out BestOnwardTicket.com for a temporary exit flight.

BONUS! The 60 days Tourist Visa can be extended an extra 30 days (equaling 90 days total)! You can extend this visa while in Thailand, starting 7 days before your visa expires.

Example: My 60 days expires on June 7th. So I can go to immigration on June 1st (or any day in-between) to renew.

To do this, go to the nearest Thai immigration office and pay an extra $60 USD/2,000 Baht along with proof of an exit flight.

These rules apply for tourists coming from western countries such as Canada, The UK, South Africa, The USA, Australia, and Ireland.

If you live elsewhere, the rules may be different for you so check your local Thai embassy website.

NERVOUS? Even I get nervous before (and during) a new trip. The secret? Turn that nervous energy into excited energy. Instead of saying *"I'm afraid to do this"* say *"I can't wait to do this"* and let life happen.

Weather for Thailand

December to April is considered the dry season with temperatures starting at 77°F (25°C) and increasing to about 102°F (35°C) towards the end of the season. Expect around 60% humidity during this season…which means you will be sticky all day.

Mid-May to September is the rainy season. The temperature will stay pretty steady around 86°F (30°C) but the rain can be unpredictable. Some weeks it will pour and some weeks you won't see more than a couple hours of rain. To save disappointment, expect a couple hours of rain every day in the afternoon during rainy season. Also, humidity can get pretty intense at around 80%.

Official Best Time to Visit: November – February

Alexa's Vote for the Best Time to Visit: Year-round

November – February is officially considered the "best" time to visit Thailand because of the dry weather and moderate temperature. This is also called "High Season".

March – October is "Low Season". Low Season has more rain and hotter temperatures but also has less people and cheaper prices!

So, don't stress if you can't make your trip fit these dates exactly. Thailand is hospitable year-round. Take advantage of the lower prices, emptier planes, and embrace the rain! In the end, you'll still get a tan.

TO SUMMARIZE

November – February (High Season)

Most pleasant temperatures

Less rain

More tourists

March – October (Off-Season)

Afternoon rain showers for 2–3 hours

Hotter and more humid

Fewer people = emptier beaches

WHEN TO VISIT & WHERE

Rule of Thumb for the BEST Weather

Krabi & Phuket	November – March
Koh Samui	February – July
Bangkok	December – February
Chiang Mai	October – January & April (avoid burning season in February/March)

PRO TIP! No, you can't drink the tap water—but it is safe to brush your teeth and bathe in!

What to Pack for Thailand

First, don't stress. As long as you have your passport, bank card and a decent backpack, you're ready for Thailand. Anything you need or forget at home can be found here.

So, no matter what you do or don't pack - you'll be just fine.

But let's take this opportunity to get organized now so you don't have to spend your vacation hunting for things you forgot.

As you know, I've been traveling for over a decade. I've got this packing thing down and here is what I recommend to my girlfriends traveling to Thailand.

WHAT TO PACK

✓ PASSPORT WITH AT LEAST 6 MONTHS VALIDITY

Some countries enforce it and some countries don't – but to play it safe, you need to have at least 6 months validity on your passport. For example, if it's January 1st, 2024, and your passport expires before June 1st, 2024, they might not let you in the country and you'll have to return home immediately.

✓ TRAVEL INSURANCE

Yes, you do need it. Everything from minor bouts of food poisoning to helicopter medevac off a mountain, a standard travel insurance policy is a non-negotiable in my (literal) book. Check your current medical insurance plan. They might already cover Thailand. If they don't, here is what I use:

✈ **World Nomads** which offers full-coverage plans for extremely reasonable prices.

✈ **SafetyWing** is also a really affordable option, especially if you're traveling long term.

✓ THE PERFECT BACKPACK OR SUITCASE

The Bag I Recommend…

The Osprey Farpoint 40 Litre Backpack ☞

It's been over 5 years that I've been using this bag. I love it so much that I just bought the exact same model again to use for another 5 years.

♥ This bag qualifies as a carry-on

♥ It's extremely comfortable to wear

♥ The open-zip style means that you can keep your clothes organized

♥ I swear it's got Mary Poppins magic because I can fit 3 months of clothes in one tiny space

 Or the **Osprey Fairview 55** that comes with a zip-on and off day bag.

✓ WALKING SHOES

Bring 3 pairs of shoes:

◇ 1 Pair of Flip Flops or Slides

◇ 1 Pair of Cute Walking Sandals

◇ 1 Pair of Hiking / Running Shoes

This is my official trifecta of shoes. Through rain, up mountains, and on long sweaty walks, they've never failed me. I replace the same pairs of shoes every year – find them in my travel store.

✓ OB TAMPONS OR A MENSTRUAL CUP

You're going to be in a bathing suit on the beach and out on the water! And if you've never used a menstrual cup, they are a game changer. Save money every month, go 12 hours with no leaks & swim with no drips.

✓ ELECTRIC ADAPTER

It's not just the socket you have to worry about, it's also the voltage. Your phone and laptop are likely not going to be compatible with the Thai outlets. REI, Target, and Amazon have cheap Universal adapters that every traveler should own.

✓ QUICK DRY TOWEL

Hostel girls! Hostels usually don't provide towels so it's nice to bring a travel towel of your own. Not a total necessity, but a quick dry (usually some kind of microfiber) towel is nice to have– especially during the rainy season when the heat isn't there to dry things quickly. Plus, it can double as your beach towel!

✓ TROPICAL WEATHER MAKEUP

Humidity is no joke. Most foundations get super greasy and eyeshadows crease like it's their job. My makeup bag is pure perfection when it comes to long-lasting, humid, tropical weather products. Check out my travel makeup collection here.

✓ MONEY CONCEAL POUCH

This credit card size pouch is used to discreetly carry cash, cards, and keys. The Velcro strap makes it easy to secure the pouch to your bra or undies for nights out on the town.

SURVIVAL GUIDE

✓ EMERGENCY MONEY SOURCE / $100 CASH US

Have a secret stash of cash and a backup credit card in case you get in a sticky situation. Keep this emergency money source separate from your other cards and cash so that if you lose your wallet, you won't lose the secret stash, too

✓ BANK CARDS

Travel with two cards – either 2 debit cards or 1 debit + 1 credit. In the case that your bank flags one card with fraudulent activity and disables it, you'll want to have a backup. If the machine eats a card, if a card gets stolen, or if you lose your purse on a night out, a backup card will make all the difference between having mom fly you home and you continuing your travels.

The cards you need are here. ☞

NOTE! If you are from the UK, check out Starling Bank. They have the best atm exchange rates and don't charge any foreign atm charges. They can also send you a replacement if you lose or break your card to anywhere in the world that has an address!

✓ EMPTY SPACE IN YOUR BAG

It took me 5 years to learn that the less stuff you have, the more free you are. You are free to pick up and move around, free to shop for souvenirs, and free from relying on porters and taxis to help you carry your luggage. Plus, you're going to need space for all that extra shopping over here.

WHAT NOT TO PACK

X Jeans
X High-heels
X Hairspray (ya won't use it)
X A Curling Iron (with this humidity…no point)
X Too Many Bras (ya won't wear em')
X A Pharmacy of Medicine (you can get it all here)

How to Budget for Thailand

How much money should I bring?

How much will I spend? What is the least amount I can spend and still see it all?

When it comes to traveling Southeast Asia, there are 3 spending routes you can take:

Budget 💵

Stay in hostels, eat local, take the super convenient minibus, and drink beer from 7-Eleven.

Balanced 💵 💵

Spend the night in a hostel and eat street food one night, then check into a beachfront resort and sip tropical cocktails the next. Or just stay middle of the road the whole way through—not too fancy but comfortable.

Bougie 💵 💵 💵

Infinity pool resorts, private boat tours, and quick flights from one beach to the next.

	BUDGET	BALANCED	BOUGIE
TOTAL PER DAY	$30	$80	$160+

All 3 of these options are possible, easy and will offer you the trip of a lifetime—as long as you plan it right.

— DAILY EXPENSES —

Thai Street Food	$1.50
Thai Restaurant	$4.00
Hamburger	$8.00
Bottle of Beer	$3.00
Cocktail	$5.00
1 Night in a Hostel	$8.00
1 Night in a Private Room	$30.00
1 Night in a Resort	$110.00+
Day Tour	$30
1 Hour Flight	$25–150
7 hour Bus	$28

Tips to Spend Less in Thailand

♥ Visit during "low season" when accommodation and flights are cheaper

♥ Go to the ATM just once a week—the ATM fees are up to $6 per transaction

♥ Get a Sim Card and download Grab Taxi

♥ Drink beer from 7-Eleven or hole in the wall bars, rather than clubs

♥ Haggle at markets and when street shopping! Start your haggling at whalf price and work your way from there.

♥ Avoid Tuk Tuk drivers and fixed-rate taxis

♥ Eat street food

Your biggest expenses will be...

🔖 Alcohol

🔖 Partying

🔖 Organized Island Tours

Everything else can be tweaked to fit your wallet.

ALEXA'S THAILAND BUDGET RULE: Remember... **The Pad Thai Rule**

Pad Thai in Thailand costs roughly $1 USD. To save money for a big trip, ask yourself "how many Pad Thais is this" before you spend.

So, about to drop $7 on mascara at Target? Well, that's 7 meals in Thailand

Seriously, you can travel SUPER cheap in Southeast Asia. And the more Pad Thai dollars you have in your pocket, the longer you can travel.

Reevaluate your spending by thinking about it in terms of your Travel Budget!

Let's Talk About Money in Thailand

What You Need To Know About Money In Thailand...

Thai currency is called **Baht** (pronounced *bot*...like robot). Both bills and coins are commonly used!

Thai Baht is pretty! Each bill has a unique color, unlike the US dollar. Familiarize yourself with these colors to make sure you don't mistakenly hand over a 1000 when you mean to hand over a 10!

- 1,000 is gray
- 500 is purple
- 100 is red
- 50 is blue
- 20 is green
- 10 is brown

SOME QUICK MONEY TIPS...

○ **You're going to need cash in Thailand!** Hotels and big restaurants may accept cards, but street food, transportation and haggling on anything requires cash-ola!

○ **Converting US dollars to BAHT with your Brain:**

30 Thai Baht = $1 USD.

○ **Download the app "XE" right now**

This is a currency converter that will help you quickly convert prices to avoid getting ripped off

○ **How much cash to bring to Thailand:** $100-$300 USD.

○ **If you use a travel ATM card (usually with no foreign transaction fees)...**

✳ Use the ATM to withdraw cash when you land. I usually take out about 3,000-5,000 baht at a time ($90 - $150 USD).

✳ Bring $100 emergency cash and store it in a separate bag than your wallet just in case something should happen to your cards.

○ **If you do not use a travel ATM card...**

➤ Bring some cash to exchange at an exchange counter. About $100-$300 USD. I don't recommend, however, carrying around more than $300 USD.

➤ After that initial cash runs out, you'll have to bite the bullet and use the ATM.

⚠ **ATM REMINDER:** Sometimes, ATMs spit out your money first and your card second, resulting in many forgotten cards! Do a 3-step check before you leave: cash, card, receipt.

NOTE: US dollars are not accepted by establishments...and if they are, that's weird and I'm sure you're about to get ripped off.

CARDS YOU SHOULD BE TRAVELING WITH
ESPECIALLY IF YOU'RE COMING TO ASIA LONG-TERM

My # 1 Travel Rule: Don't book your flight and hotels with a debit card!

☞ *Reason #1:* If your flight or trip is cancelled, you will have no trip protection and you may never see your cash again.

☞ *Reason #2:* You are literally turning down free money if you're not taking advantage of travel credit card points when booking international flights and weeks of hotels.

Use a Travel Credit Card to...

◇ Book your flight

◇ Book your hotels

◇ Pay at restaurants

What About Debit Cards?

FOR AMERICANS, open an account with Charles Schwab Bank. With Charles Schwab, I can use any ATM in the world without ATM fees. Every time you use an ATM that isn't your bank's ATM, you are charged a "foreign ATM fee" that can be $3–8 depending on where you are. Lame. But at the end of every month, Charles Schwab reimburses all foreign ATM fees.

Chase and American Express are the cards I can't live without. I explain why I love these cards here:

HEY! WANT TO TRAVEL WITH ME?
CHECK OUT GLOWUPTRAVEL.COM

Internet & Data in Thailand

Don't get stranded without internet! You need a local Thai SIM Card to access the internet and transportation apps on the islands.

No, don't get an "international plan" with your cell phone carrier from home. Your coverage will be shit and 10x more expensive. This goes for Thailand, Cambodia, and Vietnam…everywhere in Asia.

A local SIM card will be cheaper and offer better cell coverage on the islands! In Thailand, look for the companies called **dtac** or **AIS.**

You'll go to the kiosk with your passport. They will ask you how long you're staying and recommend a plan. Usually the plans are good for 1 month durations or 1 week durations. Usually, the plans are sold as 1 month unlimited with different mbps speeds (the internet speed). The basic package is enough for using apps and maps.

I use AIS and I pay around $15 USD per month.

WHERE TO BUY THESE SIM CARDS?

○ *Option 1*: **At the Airport**

The airport (any international airport in Thailand) is the most convenient place to get one. After you exit baggage claim, you'll see a counter offering SIM cards.

The price may be a bit higher (by a couple dollars) at the airport, but not a massive rip off—you're just paying a slight "convenience premium". Keep the little card they give you; it has your new phone number on the top.

○ *Option 2:* **The Mall**

Major malls like Terminal 21 or MBK Center in Bangkok and Maya Mall in Chiang Mai will have dtac or AIS stores.

Take a photo of that number, in case you lose the card.

You'll need a new SIM card in every country. Sounds like a headache, but so is having an "international plan" with no coverage.

NOTE...

Most smart phones have a "Dual Sim" so your SIM Card from home will stay in your phone for safe keeping. But if you don't have a Dual Sim slot, make sure you put your home SIM Card in a safe place. Make sure your smartphone is "unlocked". Not unlocked? Take it to your data carrier and ask them to unlock it for you. Easy.

DOWNLOAD LOCAL APPS

Thailand is connected to some awesome apps that will make your trip a lot easier and a lot cheaper if you use them!

GrabTaxi, Bolt and InDriver

These are like Uber but cheaper. Some Grabs are actual Taxis and some are private cars. You can pay cash on the taxi meter or connect your debit card to the app.

Line

The messenger app that most Thai locals use in place of WhatsApp or texting. This app works on WIFI and data for both calling and texting.

XE

Currency Conversions in an instant.

GoogleMaps Offline

You can save Google's Thailand map offline, so that even when you don't have access to Wi-Fi or data, you can still navigate.

TripIt

Whenever you get an email confirmation from a flight, hotel, or tour – forward the flight to Travefy which will organize your itinerary on your phone. Now you have your booking confirmations, flight times, address, and maps in one place!

Bumble And Tinder

I once met a Thai guy who drove a Harley Motorbike on Bumble. He showed me parts of the city I'd never have discovered without him. Plus, I felt super cool on the back of a Harley.

Link up with a local who knows all the best spots in the city or find a sightseeing partner with another traveler. Thailand is very pro-dating app.

FUN FACT! Bumble has a friend-mode called Bumble BFF where you can search for new friends to explore with!

MY FACEBOOK GROUPS TO JOIN

 The Solo Girl's Travel Community
where you can ask questions and meet other girls.

Girls in Thailand Community
to find other girls traveling to or living in Thailand.

MY FACEBOOK PAGE

 The Solo Girl's Travel Guide
Follow and Like my Facebook page to see where I'm traveling next.

Thai Food Guide

There's more to life than just Pad Thai…

Tom Yum

A spicy and sour lemongrass soup, often served with shrimp

Tom Kha Gai

Hot and sour soup with coconut & kaffir lime leaf base served with chili, mushrooms, and chicken

Gang Kiew Wan Gai

Green curry with chicken served with steamed rice

Masaman Curry

A southern Thai curry with a peanut and potato broth served with steamed rice

Khao Man Gai

Hainanese chicken and rice served with a simple chicken broth

Pad Ga Prow Moo (kai dow)

Chili basil stir-fried pork (with a fried egg on top)

Pad See Ew

Wide rice noodles stir-fried in soy sauce with broccoli and protein (chicken, seafood, pork)

Penang Curry

My #1 recommended curry dish that is sweet and fragrant with lime kaffir lime leaves, basil and coconut.

Som Tam

Green Papaya Salad with dried shrimp

Pla Kapong Neung Manao

A whole steamed bass with lemon and chili in a shallow broth, often served at the table over fire

Khao Ka Moo

Stewed, fall-off-the-bone pork leg topped with rice and rich pork broth

Kanom Tuay

Layered sweet and salty coconut dessert pre-set in tiny bowls

Kow Neuw

Sticky rice

Khao Soi

A Burmese/Laos inspired soup made with coconut milk, red curry paste, yellow egg noodles and topped with crispy wonton strips

Kanom Krok

Little fried pancakes with a crispy shell

Kow Neuw Mamuang (Mango Sticky Rice)

Sweet and salty coconut sticky rice served with fresh mango

Ok that's enough of Big Sister Mode. Let's get to the fun stuff.

Photos From Top To Bottom:

❶ *Gang Kiew Wan Gai*

❷ *Kanom Krok*

Thai Language Guide

GREETINGS

Hello	Sa-wa-dee-kah
What's your name?	Kun chêu a-rai?
How are you?	Sa-bai-dee mai?
My name is...	Rao chêu ...
Nice to meet you	Yin dee têe dâi róo jà
Bye	Bye
Thank you.	Kap Kun Kah/Kwap
You're Welcome	Yin dee

DAY TO DAY

Yes	Chai
No	Mai Chai
Can I _____?	Dai _____ mai?
No problem.	Mai Pen Rai
I don't know	Mai Ru
I don't understand	Mai Cow Jai
How do you say ___ in Thai?	Pasa Thai ... poot waa yàng-rai
Where's the toilet?	Hong nam you nai?

SHOPPING

I don't want a bag.	Mai ow tung
How much?	Tao rai?
I want	Ow…
I don't want	Mai ow…
Big	Yai
Small	Lek
I like that	Chan chok man

PRO TIP! Don't say "Ow" alone. In slang, this word alone roughly translates into "I want sex."

FOOD

I'm hungry	Chan hew
I'm full	Chan im
Water	Nam
Beer	Be-uh
Spicy	Pet
Not spicy	Mai Pet
Delicious	Aroy
Rice	Khao
Chicken	Gai
Pork	Moo
Beef	Neau
Shrimp	Goon

Fish	Plah
Coconut	Maprow
Vegetarian	Mang-sà-wí-rát

EMERGENCY PHRASES

Leave me alone	Yā yung kap chan!
Help!	Chuay Duay!
Fire!	Fai mâi!
Stop!	Yut!

IMPORTANT

●━━━━━●

Girls end every phrase with: *Kah*

Boys end every phrase with: *Kap*

●━━━━━●

TRAVEL NOTES:

....

....

....

....

Transporation in Thailand

Thailand is easy to get around! Whether you're navigating within the city or between islands, you can get just about anywhere you want to go.

Use **12go.asia** to book your transport for just about everything.

Within each chapter, I will be describing the best ways to move about each city and island. But to appease your curiosity (or if you're like me, your anxiety), I'll give you a quick overview of transportation here.

Here's how to bop around Thailand…

Air

Plane rides are cheap and fast in Thailand. The longest part of your journey is usually getting to and from the airport! Airlines like AirAsia, Nok Air, Thai Airways and Bangkok Airways offer cheap flights around the country...but they will absolutely charge you for baggage at the airport if you haven't already purchased baggage online. Check out flights on **SkyScanner.**

Trains

The overnight train from Bangkok to Chiang Mai is a must-do experience in Thailand! Beyond that specific route, Thailand's train system is very well connected with lines that travel from the north to the south. Did I mention they are affordable and comfortable? I'm talking like $30 USD for a 12-hour ride in a comfy sleeper bed! I love the trains in Thailand!

ThailandTrains.com is a great resource to show you routes and maps throughout the country.

Boats

Longtail boats are like water taxis that zip you from beach to beach, and speed ferries take you between islands. There are dozens of companies running every route you can possibly imagine!

Tuk Tuks

As you'll read in this guide, Tuk Tuks are usually used as neighborhood transportation for locals coming home from the market or getting off the MRT. Tuk Tuks are also used as a shiny luer for tourists! And hey, I think everyone should ride in a Tuk Tuk at least once or twice in Thailand, but don't use them as your regular mode of transportation for long distances.

Grab Taxi

Just like Uber, you can use GrabTaxi! You have the option of ordering a car or a motorbike taxi (just remember to wear the helmet)!

Taxi

Metered taxis are okay to use as long as they turn on the meter! In Bangkok, it can be hard to wave down a taxi at peak hours, which is why you have option 1.

Motorbike Taxi

In the urban neighborhoods of Thailand (especially Bangkok), you'll see motorbike taxis driving around, usually wearing an orange vest. You can flag them down and hop on the back of their bike for around 10-20 baht rides around your area. You can also find the motorbike taxi stand that all the motorbike drivers use as their hub.

Mini Bus

The mini bus is one of the most convenient ways to travel long distances on a budget. When I was backpacking, I would often take the 10-hour mini bus from Bangkok to Surat Thani Town before heading over to Koh Samui. Just know, these buses get packed and the drivers can drive like maniacs.

Songthaew

Imagine a pick-up truck with benches in the back seat used as a collective form of transportation. This is a Songthaew which is used in specific regions, Chiang Mai being one. As you'll read later, Songthaews usually have a fixed price for going certain distances. You tell the driver where you're going and he'll drop you there. Or around there. Feel free to insist he point out your location if you don't know where it is. This will make sure that he's not just trying to get rid of you two blocks before your destination.

PHILIPP L. WESCHE

Big Buses

You can take a big comfy bus on long distances, like from Bangkok to Cambodia, where you'll experience aircon, free snacks and TV entertainment.

Or you can take a big bus around the city of Bangkok or between cities (like Bangkok to Pattaya to go eat chicken wings at Hooters) but those buses won't be as fancy. Either way, they're both affordable and convenient.

Bangkok Skytrain and Subway

You'll read all about this in the Bangkok chapter!

Motorbike Rentals

Don't know how to ride a scooter? I only recommend learning in calm, flat places like parts of Chiang Mai, Koh Lanta or Surat Thani town.

I learned how to ride in Surat Thani Town where my Thai friend, X, gave me lessons. Check him out here. ☞

I do not suggest learning how to ride a scooter in mountainous areas, party islands or big cities. It won't go well. For example, you will walk around islands like Koh Tao where you'll see people walking around bandaged up like mummies on Halloween. Thailand's traffic can be chaotic and the topography is hilly! Walk your cute butt around rather than learning how to ride a scooter on vacation.

Already know how to ride a scooter? Now, you just need to practice weaving through traffic and narrow alleyways.

MOTORBIKE PROTIPS!

◊ Wear a helmet! Police can fine you if they spot you driving without one.

◊ Keep your purse in front of you while driving and do not use your smartphone while riding on the back of a bike.

◊ Take pictures of the motorbike before you rent it. Take photos of any scratches or damages so you won't be held liable. Take a photo of the license plate, too, so you don't lose it!

◊ American? Go to AAA to get an international drivers' license for $20. No test. Just your passport, 2 passport photos and 20- minutes needed.

◊ Also also, if the Police catch you driving without an international drivers' license (not a common occurrence), they may ask for a bribe. Try to convince them that you only have 100 baht. They'll eventually accept it and let you leave.

Safe Girl Tips & Advice

THAI DO'S & DONT'S

Girl, you're grown. I know. But I'll just leave these here in case you're interested....

PLEASE DO...

♥ Wai

To show respect to your elders, monks, and friends, put your hands in prayer at your chin and give a slight bow of the head—this is a wai. You'll start to love it.

♥ Cover your Shoulders & Knees in the Temples

Modesty is required inside spiritual spaces. Wear a long skirt or buy a Thai shawl to wrap around your waist and/or shoulders when you visit the temples.

♥ Smile

In tense or unfair situations, argue with a smile. Thais don't like to "lose face" or get embarrassed. You're much more likely to resolve an issue with a smile.

♥ Learn to Speak a Little Thai

You'd be amazed by how far a little language goes. You can haggle cheaper prices, order the right food, and make friends! Use the app called Memrise to learn key phrases

♥ Tip Your Salon Lady

Massages, pedicures, haircuts—these kinds of services definitely deserve a tip. 15—20% should do it.

PLEASE DON'T...

✗ Disrespect the King

This one is a super don't. Thailand loves their king—he was a great man who did a lot for this country. Speaking disrespectfully about him is unheard of.

✗ Show the Bottom of your Feet

In Thailand, feet are seen to be lowly as they are connected to the ground where human suffering occurs. Don't step over people sitting on the ground, don't point the bottom of your feet towards Thais while sitting cross-legged, and don't don't don't rest your feet up on a chair or on a seat in the bus.

✗ Wear Bikinis in Public

I know you're on vacation, but Thai People are not. Save your banging bod for the beach or pool and cover up while you walk around town.

✗ Try to Buy anything Illegal

If you go looking for trouble in Thailand, you'll find it. While you might meet travelers with stories of getting high and taking trippy substances, they are all lucky they didn't get caught. Just because drugs are readily available, doesn't mean they're risk-free. Law enforcement is heavily cracking down on partying in Thailand (but often looks the other way for Full Moon Parties). Respect the laws of the country.

✗ Hook Up in Public

Vacation romances are half the fun of traveling. Holding hands and some kissing is cool, but save the make out sessions for a private space.

✗ Tip Taxis or Servers

I mean, you can if you want to. But typically, Thais don't tip. In some situations, tipping is actually quite awkward.

✗ Touch a Monk

No one—not me, not you, not the Pope—can touch a monk. No handshakes, no selfies and no hugs. Instead, smile and wai.

ACTIVITIES TO AVOID

Just because you can do it, doesn't mean you should do it…

X Ping Pong Shows

More traumatizing than entertaining, Ping Pong Shows are where women stick objects and animals inside themselves and perform tricks on stage. If you're out of touch, you may get a rush from how shocking this is to watch. But if you're plugged into reality, you'll likely be horrified for these exploited women who feel that Ping Pong shows are their only opportunity for work. There will be plenty of Thai hawkers inviting you Ping Pong shows while you walk around touristy areas—just ignore them and walk along. Purchasing a ticket is perpetuating a disgusting industry.

X Tattoos of Buddha

Buddha is sacred in these parts. So much so, that in neighboring Myanmar, a backpacker was jailed for having a tattoo of Buddha. That is quite unlikely to happen to you in Thailand, but it goes to show how disrespectful it is.

X Riding Elephants

What may seem like a 'Bucket List' activity is actually an industry bred out of animal cruelty and torture. Instead of riding elephants, find an elephant sanctuary that allows you to feed, trek and bathe in the river with elephants rescued from the circus, work camps and elephant riding tourist centers around Thailand.

X Tiger Temples

Those cute baby tigers that you're about to take a photo with…do you ever wonder where they come from? Tigers are essentially farmed, taken from their mothers at 2 weeks old, and given to tourists to bottle feed. And that's only the beginning…

ALEXA'S PRO TIPS!

If you go into Thailand knowing nothing but these tips, know that you'll be instantly be lightyears ahead of every other tourist here.

♥ Beer, Wine & Alcohol Sale Times

Alcohol is sold between 11am–2pm & 5pm–11pm. This goes for all supermarkets and convenient stores. However, if you can find a little Mom & Pop shop—they'll hook you up 24/7.

♥ Use Airbnb Experience Tours!

Food tours. Cooking classes. Tuk Tuk adventures. Walking tours. A photographer that will show you and shoot you at the most beautiful locations! Forget tour companies! Link up with a local offering to show you around their backyard. Airbnb Tours are professionally run for amazing prices and the profits go directly to those who deserve em.

♥ Toasties

Curry is good but 7-11 Toasties are better. Grab one of these sandwiches from the fridge section of 7-11 and hand it to the 7-11 staff who will cook it for you. The ham and cheese croissant is my favorite! Warning: these treats are addictive!

♥ Ask for "No Sugar"

Thai's love processed sugar (obesity is becoming a national crisis here). They put heaps of sugar into fresh fruit smoothies, coffee, tea, and will even add a tablespoon of sugar to your noodle soup and pad thai. I find myself asking for no sugar nearly every time I order something—no matter what it is. If you like your food fresh, don't feel weird doing the same.

☞ *I don't wan't sugar:* Mai ow nam taan

♥ Bumble

Find a sightseeing partner with another traveler or link up with a local who knows all the best spots in the city. This is a very date-friendly country. Just avoid Tinder…it's more popular for illicit dating…

♥ Carry On Bags

When you go to check-in to your domestic flight within Thailand or smaller Asian airlines to leave Thailand (like AirAsia, Nok Air, Thai Lion, etc) the airline attendant will likely weigh your carry-on bag. If it is over 7kg (15lbs), you will have to pay around $60 to check it.

So, pack light or distribute your weight between your "personal bag" and carry-on bag before you approach the check-in desk. Alternatively, just pay the checked bag fee when you book your ticket. The price is much much cheaper online.

♥ Carry Passport Photos

If you're country hopping, get cheap passport photos made in Thailand and carry them around in your wallet. This will save you time and money during border crossings.

♥ Keep in Mind

ATMs in Thailand spit out your money first and your card second, resulting in many a forgotten card.

♥ Practice the Safe Code BEFORE Locking the Safe

Before you put your belongings in your room's safe, practice the code. You can reset a safe code with the button inside the safe, near the hinge of the door. Always reset the safe, enter you pin and then practice opening and closing the safe a couple of times before you lock your stuff in there. OH and make sure the safe keys aren't INSIDE the safe.

FEELING NERVOUS AND NEED A PEP TALK?

Want to go over your itinerary? Want me to help you pick hotels? Have more questions?

Call me. You + Me + 20 minutes on video chat = The best trip ever without all the scary stuff.

Go to calendly.com/alexawest/travelchats. Or scan here to schedule your call ☞

SAFE GIRL TIPS FOR THAILAND

A quick briefing...

⚠ Violent crime against tourists is rare.

⚠ Crime here typically comes in the form of scams rather than actual violence.

⚠ The biggest danger is motorbike accidents

⚠ Assaults typically happen between two travelers, rather than a traveler and a local.

⚠ Use street smarts like you would back home and you'll be fine.

✓ Wear a Cross Shoulder Bag

Aggressive theft is not an issue over here. No one will run up to you, snatch your bag and run away (although...monkeys totally will). But if your bag is hanging loosely by your side, wandering hands can find a way to snatch your stuff (particularly on the islands).

Wearing a cross-shoulder bag is the best way to keep your belongings secure and is an assurance that you won't take your bag off to place it by your feet, on the table, or the chair beside youbecause that's another place where it can get swiped, and you won't even notice.

This is my favorite cross-shoulder bag for traveling. ☞

Again, petty theft is most popular in tourist party areas like Koh Phangan or Koh Phi Phi.

✓ Cheap Alcohol = "Fake" Alcohol = Wicked Hangover

It's a common scam: Thai bars will fill brand-named bottles with homemade alcohol that is wickedly strong.

If you see "too good to be true" drink specials like "5 shots for 100 baht" or seriously cheap cocktails – beware. These places aren't using the good stuff.

While you're not likely to experience liver failure after one of these homemade drinks, you are certainly going to experience an intense hangover and an increased likelihood of blacking out. Stick to beer – unless you're drinking at a reputable hotel or hostel.

FYI: You can trust the cheap alcohol served at the hostels in this book. Bodega, Mad Monkey, Lub D – they are all serving the real stuff.

✓ Beware Of Sneaky Bartenders

When paying bartenders, make sure you say out loud "Here's 1000" or "500" to make sure they can't claim that you paid a lesser amount – which they've been known to do in party areas with the hopes that you're too drunk to notice what you gave them.

✓ Let's Talk about Sexual Assault

Foreign women (that's us) are statistically more likely to be sexually assaulted by a foreign man (other travelers) on holiday than they are to be sexually assaulted by a Thai man. Think about it; in hostels, hotels and bars- we are more likely to be hanging around foreign men, quite possibly with alcohol in our systems, and therefore exposed to that risk. Just like you would at home, monitor your sobriety levels and be aware of your surroundings.

To be even safer, insist on female massage therapists when going to an unfamiliar massage spot.

✓ Look Both Ways Before You Cross the Street

Duh, but really- traffic here is different than back home. Pedestrians don't have the right of way here- even on a green light. When crossing the street, don't just look for cars. Also, look for motorbikes that whiz between the cars.

✓ Drive Super Carefully

With bikes and booze, comes the fast, furious and idiotic. One false move after two drinks too many, your tire slips in the dust and bam – accident. Even if you think that you're okay after a few drinks, it's the other reckless idiots you've got to watch out for. You need quick reaction times to avoid drunk drivers after sunset – so keep all of your wits about you by driving totally sober.

✓ Walking at Night

Make smart choices. Stay on lit roads, don't walk down a dark beach late at night, walk with a friend when possible, and don't get super drunk and wander off by yourself. Follow those common sense rules, and you'll be safe as can be.

✓ Pick your ATMs Wisely

As a universal travel rule, random ATMs on the side of the road can be sketchy. ATMs inside convenience stores, inside bank kiosks (human-sized glass boxes) or inside of a bank are your best insurance policies against becoming a victim of ATM skimming or having a wad of cash ripped out of your hand - although, I've never heard of either of these happening in Thailand.

✓ AirBnbs

AirBnb is 'technically' illegal in Thailand – but that doesn't stop hosts or guests from using AirBnb. Basically, condo buildings and condo tenants simply don't want their place turning into a party hotel.

So, be low key at your AirBnb and if anyone asks, you're "staying with a friend." Don't throw a pool party and don't "check in" at reception – and you will be undetected. Your hosts will arrange everything with you beforehand. And no, you cannot go to jail for this. Worst case, the AirBnb host gets a warning from the building.

✓ Gem & Jewelry Store Scams

In Bangkok, the most common scam is one where a tuk tuk or taxi driver takes you to a jewelry store where they get commission if you buy. It's annoying and a waste of time, but not dangerous.

⚠ **"Closed today" Declarations:** If you want to go to a temple and the Tuk Tuk driver tells you that the temple is closed or opening late today due to a "Buddhist Holiday" …they're lying and are trying to get you to a jewelry store.

⚠ **20 Baht Rides:** If a taxi driver offers you a suspiciously low rate for a day of sightseeing, expect to pass all the tourist destinations and be taken straight to a jewelry store.

In general, us foreign women can expect to feel safe in Thailand as long as we use common sense and don't get too wasted…

✔ Always Prioritize Your Comfort Over Being Polite

I decided to try a new massage place in Bangkok today. I walked in and was greeted by the nicest old man ever. He changed my shoes and as I began walking towards the back, I realized that all the massage therapists were male – a very strange sight in Thailand.

And then I noticed that all the clients were male. And then it clicked: this massage shop doubles as a gay massage parlor.

5 years ago, I would have gone along with the massage in order to be polite, all while subjecting my body and my mind to a very uncomfortable situation for an hour...while naked… JUST TO BE POLITE. But not today. Today, I simply stopped, smiled, turned around and gracefully left. No harm done. No one's feelings hurt. No fucks given.

I have a laundry list of uncomfortable and dangerous positions that I have put myself in while traveling in the past… just to avoid embarrassing myself or avoid being rude.

Us women are conditioned to be polite, and it's time we stop.

Remember: Comfort first, manners second.

Now! No more stressing. You've got all the information you need to travel safely. You can handle this. Tell your anxiety to fuck off.

CHAPTER ONE

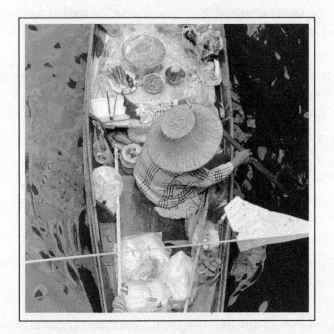

Bangkok

———— ◆ ————

BEST FOR:

Exploring temples, discovering hidden markets, and eating the
most incredible local food

DAYS NEEDED:

3 nights minimum

———— ◆ ————

CHAPTER ONE

Bangkok

I'll admit it. I wasn't impressed with Bangkok the first 12 times I visited. It felt big and busy and overwhelming- because it is.

For years, I stuck to the heavily trodden tourist path with high prices, jaded locals and fellow travelers who were just as clueless as I was. Because that's easy to find.

I never knew about the hidden night markets where only locals go. I didn't know about the glamorous sky bars with glittering views of the city. And I certainly didn't know how to get off the tourist path and start exploring the real Bangkok

Then, my brother who was also living in Bangkok, got a Thai girlfriend and the whole world opened up to us! Koby (which means frog in Thai) yanked us all around Bangkok and showed me layers of her city that I never would have found without her. But thanks to Koby, I fell in love with the real Bangkok! And you're about to, too.

Bangkok is the capital city of Thailand where over 8 million Thais and expats call home. With a mix of modern and old-school culture, the adventures are literally endless.

Stay at an upscale hotel where you spend your days with Thai massages and cooking classes by day, then hop from one glamorous rooftop bar to the other at night.

Traveling on a budget? Stay on Khao San Road where you can mingle with other backpackers in cozy guest houses and rowdy hostels, go on day trips to amazing Buddhist temples, and spend the night wandering night markets sampling the most delicious $1 bites

As you're about to discover, a trip to Bangkok is completely customizable for any and every budget. Don't skip this city. You'll later be able to tell other Bangkok haters that they don't know what they're talking about.

AREAS TO KNOW IN BANGKOK

Bangkok is huge, ya'll. But at the same time, it's accessible. In this section, I'm going to help you mentally understand the breakdown of Bangkok's neighborhood so you can decide where you want to stay or explore.

Typically, on a 1-week vacation to Bangkok, there are two areas you are going to explore:

1. **Khao San Road Area & Chinatown**
2. **Sukhumvit Road**

1 KHAO SAN ROAD

Besides the party, Khao San Road is just a stone's throw away from every iconic historical and cultural landmark in Bangkok. There's nowhere more suitable to discover the Thai way of life, which is precisely how Khao San Road came to be backpacker central.

Khao San Road is the oldest backpacker street in the world, born way back in the 70's when explorers would arrive in Bangkok after a long trip to Nepal or Vietnam, throw their backpacks down and swap stories with strangers over cold beers and scorpions on a stick. Khao San has always been wild.

I first started traveling to Bangkok back in the days of clicky-phones. Khao San Road still served as the gate to the rest of Southeast Asia. With no apps or smart phones, you'd come to Khao San Road in person and visit the tour agencies that would arrange your buses, minivans and trains to the next adventure.

All Khao San Road has been and known for the past 50 years is tourism brought by waves of travelers from all over the world. And Khao San Road is still the hub for travelers in Bangkok…but things are slowly changing.

While you'll still find bars with live music, cheap drinks and scorpions on a stick… this street not what it used to be. During COVID, the Thai government pivoted their Khao San Road initiatives from nurturing backpackers to entertaining Thai college kids. What's the difference? Backpackers like an atmosphere that is raw and rough-around-the-edges whereas Thai students like modern spaces with western facades. We want old, they want new. The unfortunate result here is that lots of mom-and-pop stalls on Khao San road have been torn down and replaced with sterile chain restaurants. The old bars were replaced with nightclubs blasting music to compete with the nightclub next door.

But the good news is that the street next to Khao San Road, Rambuttri Road, is the new Khao San. It's still intact with mom-and-pop restaurants, food carts and little shopping stalls. In fact, the very end of Rambuttri Road is a foodie night market, authentic as can be! This is where you want to go now.

Please do give Khao San Road a walk-through; you'll likely find some stalls and bars that interest you (as long as you're not expecting the old Khao San) but then head to the Rambuttri Road which stretches from the night market down across Samsen Road and keeps going.

You'll still find countless stalls lined along the winding streets selling clothing, jewelry, luggage, electronics, souvenirs and knick-knacks galore - all at super reasonable prices, especially if you haggle! There are massages to be had, both street food and restaurant dishes to be eaten, and people watching to be done. Once nightfall rolls around, this area turns into one entertaining circus filled with tipsy backpackers from every walk of life. You can still find the Khao San vibe if you know where to look.

Highlights:
★ This area is surrounded by amazing places to stay, sleep and meet other travelers!
★ You can walk or tuk tuk just about everywhere including to the Grand Palace.
★ Many transportation operators make Khao San Road an easy jumping off spot to reach the rest of the country.

↻ *How to Get There:* Stay in the area or take a taxi from BTS Victory Monument (less traffic this way)

CHINA TOWN / YAOWARAT

If you're hungry for out of this world seafood, go to China Town or "Yaowarat". If you're looking for exotic herbs and spices, go to China Town. If you're wanting to take photos of bizarre dark alleys with vendors selling an array of cured meats, go to China Town. If you're looking for Eastern medicine being sold in the spirit of ancient tradition, go to China Town. You could easily spend a whole day walking the streets lined with food stalls, taking photos of historic buildings that date back to 1902, or getting a taste of the Thai-Chinese culture fusion.

In terms of temples, there's Wat Traimit- a temple that is home to the world's largest Gold Buddha, and Wat Mangkol Kamalawat- the principal Buddhist temple for religious celebrations in the area.

PRO TIP! China Town is right next to the train station Hua Lamphong. Make a visit before catching your train!

☾ How to Get There:

○ **Option 1:** Take a water taxi to Ratchawong Pier and walk a couple hundred meters to Yaowarat Road and Sampeng Lane

○ **Option 2:** Take a Taxi

○ **Option 3:** Take the MRT to Hua Lamphong Station (Chinatown) and take a taxi towards Yaowarat Road

TRUE STATEMENT:
Most travelers come to Khao San Road and think that is all there is to Bangkok! For my first 2 years in Thailand, I sincerely thought Khao San Road was the center of the city and there was no more to explore beyond this point...but I couldn't have been more wrong!

❷ SUKHUMVIT - THE TRUE CITY CENTER

Sukhumvit Road is the main vein of city life for locals and expats living in Bangkok. The BTS Skytrain runs along Sukhumvit making it very convenient to explore each (very different) neighborhood.

Along Sukhumvit, here are some of my favorite neighborhoods. You have...

ARI

The more trendy neighborhood for both Thais and expats! This neighborhood has a modern mall and some bougie restaurants, but still holds its local flavor with some of the best street food in the area. Ari is a good place to stay if you plan to take a bus to Cambodia or explore Chatuchak Market.

☾ How to Get There: BTS Ari

VICTORY MONUMENT

Honestly, most Thais don't even know what the monument at Victory Monument is all about. The answer: it's an ode to the Thai military. However, this monument is not what makes Victory Monument such an inviting destination. Actually, Thais and Farang know Victory Monument as a street shopping haven with tons of makeup stalls (my favorite), Thai clothing stalls, food stalls, and collection of mini malls while also being a major traffic hub for the city where you can catch minivans to other provinces. While there aren't as many minivan travel options as there used to be, Victory Monument is conveniently located on the BTS and is home to many important public buses- including the airport bus.

↻ *How to Get There:* BTS *Victory Monument*

SILOM

Silom area is home to Patpong- the other Red Light district which is full of Ping Pong shows, male strip clubs, and if you've got the eye to spot em- drug dealers. While this may sound super scary and unsafe, it isn't. This is simply just another side to Bangkok that may or may not intrigue you.

At night, Silom is brightly lit with a large market where you can buy scarves and souvenirs or take it easy at one of the bars that line the street offering mixers at great prices. Worth a look-see!

↻ *How to Get There:* BTS *Silom*

PRO TIP! *Many entertainment hawkers will offer you a "free five-minute" peek of a male strip show but remember that nothing is ever free in Thailand. They'll likely find a way to pinch some money off of you.*

CHIT LOM AND SIAM

These two BTS stops are right next to each other and are best known as the bougie shopping districts with the big malls! Here, you can find fancy stores like Prada, western stores like H&M and all the fast food you've been missing. You can also visit the Erawan Shrine here (or peek down at it from the sky bridge while you walk between the two stops). Want to shop like a Thai? One of the biggest Thai Malls is also located in this area, it's called Platinum Mall - and it has the best deals on souvenirs, clothes and shoes...as long as you're ready to hunt.

NANA

The Red Light district that has some of the best people watching at night. You'll find cheap drinks and lots of fantastic middle eastern food. Oh, and a Hooters.

ASOKE

You can consider Askoke to be central Sukhumvit, home to Terminal 21 Shopping mall. This mall is worth a visit just for the amazing food court, alone. But they also have a movie theater which is a lifesaver when you want to escape the Bangkok heat. Askoke is also a cross section for the MRT underground subway. At night, walk over to Soi Cowboy, the shocking girly-bar street. More about Soi Cowboy on page 92.

THONG LOR

Come here to Octave Rooftop Bar on the top of the Marriott Hotel, but first, go to Soi 38 Night Market. This area is lined with some great street food spots.

THE NEIGHBORHOOD OF SAMRONG

Ever wonder what Bangkok looked like 20 years ago before the development boom? Samrong will show you. Visit an area untouched by westerners where locals are genuinely surprised to see you. Home to the biggest open-air market in Bangkok, you can taste the freshest fruits and veggies, eat lunch at local curry pots, get foot massages for less than 200 baht and find herbs and tea for the lowest prices. Just be prepared for people staring at the pretty 'Farang' girl. The locals here are farmers and factory workers who haven't been exposed much to the western world, and will greet you with huge smiles.

PRO TIP! Take the stairs outside of Big C Shopping center that lead down to basement level where there's an underground alley that wraps around the center. You'll find my 2 favorite massage shops in the city for foot massages and Thai massage the way locals like em'.

↻How to Get There: *BTS Samrong (located after BTS Bearing- some BTS maps don't show this stop because it's so new- but it exists).*

❷ Where Should You Stay?

If you're looking to meet people, I'd say stay in Khao San and venture over to Sukhumvit for an afternoon and evening.

If you're looking to explore the real city of Bangkok and aren't afraid of public transportation, stay in Sukhumvit and venture over to Khao San for an afternoon and evening. Or, do both! Half-half your stay now that you know both areas exist!

Personally, I tell my friends to stay in Khao San Road first - for at least 3 nights. If they have more time, I say to move to Sukhumvit. Often your trip

will begin and end in Bangkok so another way to do it is to stay in Khao San on arrival to Bangkok, and stay in Sukhumvit when you're coming back to Bangkok.

There are, of course, a million more worlds packed into Bangkok that I didn't mention here - but you will find bigger bites of the Bangkok universe sprinkled throughout this next chapter....

Bonus Bangkok Area: BANG KRACHAO

Escape the city for some fresh air in what is called "The Lungs of Bangkok". There, you can rent a bike and explore park after park nestled amongst groves of palm trees, aquatic plants, botanical gardens, and ponds filled with wildlife. Wooden bridges and a tall tower offer spectacular views- so bring your camera.

Also accessible by bike, explore the Incense & Herbal House, the Fighting Fish Gallery or the Amphawa Floating Market (not so many boats, but a seemingly infinite amount of market stalls). Not many tourists know about this park so enjoy the open space- open every day from 6am-8pm.

ↄ*How to Get There:* Take a water taxi to Klong Toey Pier. When you get to land, rent a bike from there
✳ *Best Days to Visit:* Saturday and Sunday when the floating market is open! You can reach all of the Sukhumvit area on the sky train, or cross over to the underground MRT at Asoke.

In both areas of town, Khao San and Sukhumvit, you can find cheap hotels and food - and you can also find fancy hotels and food.

FUN THAI FACT!
Bangkok has the longest name of any city in the world, but locals call it 'Krungthep' or 'City of Angels' in English.

Getting into Bangkok

First things first, let's get you into town…

✈ FROM SUVARNABHUMI AIRPORT (BKK/SVB)

○ Option 1: Arrange a Car in Advance

Get off the plane and have a driver waiting for you with your name on a sign. It's not as expensive as you think!

📍 *Destination:* Anywhere.
📍 *Where:* They'll be waiting for your fancy ass as soon as you enter the arrival hall.
💸 *How Much:* Private cars start at $20 USD

Book here:

○ Option 2: Grab Taxi

Just like Uber, have a car pick you up on the curb. Download the app, connect to airport WiFi, type in your address and go.

📍 *Destination:* Anywhere.
📍 *Where:* Pretend your mom is picking you up from the airport, where would you meet her? Follow the signs for curb pick up.
💸 *How Much:* 250–600 Baht depending on where you're going.
🕐 *How Long:* Typically, 45 minutes to 1 hour, depending on traffic.
🕐 *Times of Operation:* 24/7

○ Option 3: Metered Taxi

📍 *Destination:* Sukhumvit, Khao San Road, and beyond!
📍 *Where:* On level 1, one level below the Arrivals Hall.
💸 *How Much:* The taximeter operates by distance with a metered fare. On this journey, you'll also pay a 70 Baht freeway tax and a 50 Baht airport tax. In

total, the ride will cost somewhere 250–600 Baht depending on the location of your accommodation.

🕓 *How Long:* Typically, 45 minutes to 1 hour, depending on traffic

⚠ Sometimes taxi drivers will ask you if you want to take the freeway instead of the main road—as it really does save a lot of time sitting in the horrid Sukhumvit traffic.

⚠ Avoid the private Taxi kiosks inside the airport! If someone is yelling "Taxi, taxi, where you go?"—keep on walking! These companies offer flat-fare (instead of metered) taxi rates. Their prices will easily be twice as high.

○ Option 4: Skytrain Airport Link

📍 *Destination:* Sukhumvit and beyond.
📍 *Where:* Access the Airport Link inside the airport on the basement level by following the signs that hang outside the arrival gate. The link makes several stops, two of which connect to the BTS and MRT.

☞ Makkasan for MRT
☞ Phaya Thai for BTS

Once at the MRT, you can hop on the train bound for Chinatown & the Grand Palace. This stop is called Sanam Chai. This stop is also very well known for being the most beautiful MRT stop in Bangkok.

💰 *How Much:* You'll pay between 15–55 Baht depending on the stop.
🕓 *How Long:* The sky train departs every 15 minutes and takes 25 minutes for the whole distance, beginning to end.
🕓 *Times of Operation:* The Airport Link runs from 6am–Midnight.

○ Option 5: Take a Bus

The Airport Express runs on 4 different routes throughout the city towards major hotels.

📍 *Destination:* Sukhumvit, Khao San Road, and beyond!
📍 *Where:* You'll find the official Airport Express Counter on level 1 near Exit 8. The busses are big and air conditioned!

🎫 *How Much:* 150 Baht per person.

⊙ *How Long:* Typically 45 minutes to 1 hour, depending on traffic.

⊙ *Times of Operation:* Buses leave every hour from 5am–Midnight.

✈ FROM DON MUEANG AIRPORT (DMK)

○ Option 1: Arrange a Car in Advance

Like your dad is coming to pick you up...but you've never met him before. A dude will be waiting at the airport, help you carry your luggage to the car and get you safely to your hotel.

📍 *Destination:* Anywhere.

📍 *Where:* They'll be waiting for you with your name on a sign in the arrival hall.

🎫 *How Much:* Private cars start at $20 USD

Book here:

○ Option 2: Grab Taxi

The same as an Uber! Download the app, type in your address and go.

📍 *Destination:* Anywhere.

📍 *Where:* Meet at curb-side pick0-up. I usually message them what gate (number above the door) that I'm standing outside of.

🎫 *How Much:* 250–600 Baht depending on where you're going. If there is traffic, the driver might ask you if it's okay to use the tollway (I usually just say yes) and then it will be an extra 125 Baht in tolls.

⊙ *How Long:* Typically, 45 minutes to 1 hour, depending on traffic.

○ Option 3: Metered Taxi

📍 *Destination:* Sukhumvit, Khao San Road, and beyond!

📍 *Where:* You will find metered taxis on level 1. Walk out of the arrival gate all the way to the left end of the hall where you'll see the line for metered taxis.

🎫 *How Much:* The taximeter operates by distance with a metered fare. You'll pay a 50 Baht freeway and airport tax of 50 Baht. In total, the ride will cost somewhere 250–600 Baht depending on the location of your accommodation.

☞ Sometimes the taxis will ask you if you want to take the freeway instead of the main road—as it really does save a lot of time sitting in the horrid Sukhumvit traffic.

☞ Avoid the private purple Taxi kiosks in the airport! If someone is yelling "Taxi, taxi, where you go?"—keep on walking! These companies offer flat-fare (instead of metered) taxi rates. Their prices will easily be twice as high.

☉ *How Long:* Typically, 45 minutes to 1 hour, depending on traffic.

○ Option 4: Take a Bus

The cheapest option!

♥ *Destination:* Sukhumvit Road, Khao San Road and the BTS/MRT.

PRO TIP: Headed to Khao San Road? Take the bus to the MRT train line then, hop on the MRT and head towards Sanam Chai station, next to the Grand Palace in the Khao San Road area.

♥ *Where:* Walk through the arrival gate and walk outside (Level 2). You'll see signs advertising Bus A and Bus B—usually with a beaten down red bus in front of the signs.

💰 *How Much:* The bus fare is around 30 Baht per person and the buses leave every 30 minutes, 24 hours a day!

☉ *How Long:* Typically, 45 minutes to 1 hour, depending on traffic.

PRO TIP! Make sure you have 100 Baht notes or smaller, as the ticket lady cannot break big bills!

Bus A and Bus B stop near stations for the BTS and MRT along Sukhumvit Road. You can hop off and connect to the BTS or MRT, or head to your hotel by jumping in a Taxi.

Here are the BTS and MRT stops made by airport buses:

Bus A1	BTS Mo Chit > BTS/MRT Chatuchak
Bus A2	BTS Chatuchak > BTS Mo Chit > BTS Saphan Kwai > BTS Ari > BTS Sanam Pao > BTS Victory Monument
Bus A4	Yommarat > Lan Luang > Phan Fa > Democracy Monument > Wat Bowonniwet > Khao San Road > Sanam Luang

The bus attendant will announce the stops, but don't be shy to confirm which stop is yours by asking the ticket attendant or other local riders around you.

AIRPORT PRO TIP!

Take 10 minutes and purchase a Sim Card with internet data before you leave the Airport. It's a time and stress-saver!

You can get plans that last for 3 days, 1 week, 1 month, etc., starting as low as $8. This will be a big help in getting to your accommodation and getting around the city for the rest of your trip.

✎ **JOURNAL PROMPT**

What I'm looking forward to the most in Thailand...

....

....

....

....

Where to Stay in Bangkok

I have a slight hotel obsession, and it started in Bangkok. Know that I have chosen the absolute best hotel options for every budget and mood. I can't wait to show you...

KHAO SAN AREA

Old Capital Bike Inn

My #1 choice for Bangkok guest houses. Old Capital Bike Inn represents history, architecture, culture, food, comfort...and bathtubs. I've never been more romanced by a hotel. When you stay here, you are seen. You're not just another backpacker, you're their special guest and you will be taken care of.

Old Capital Bike Inn is run by Jason, a Bangkok boy who has taken an old shop house which has been in his family for several generations and renovated it in the most dazzling way, paying homage to his heritage while providing a luxury experience for you. I can't speak highly enough of this gem, its location near the must-see sights, the personal recommendations Jason delivered (which led me to local bars and flower markets), the most enchanting breakfasts, free vintage bike rentals or the fact that Jason leads complimentary bicycle tours that take you through hidden parts of Bangkok off the tourist path. This isn't just a stay, it's a welcome to Thailand and an unforgettable experience. ***Bonus!*** Staying here, you get access to a pool nearby!

★**Style:** Privates Rooms
💸**Budget:** $$
📍**Where:** Old Town, just a 12-minute
walk to Khao San Area

❤**Room Recommendation:** Suite with Garden Terrace   **BOOK HERE**

. . . .

Inn a Day

Located in what I call "True Bangkok", Inn a Day will leave you speechless. The rooms feel like a modern-day art gallery. Go to sleep with views of the regal Wat Po from your bed, and wake up with a coffee on your patio while watching the water taxis zip by. With its close proximity to the Grand Palace, Reclining Buddha, Saranrom Park, Wang Long Market, and Khao San Road - this is the ultimate sightseeing hotel. Ps. On my last trip to Bangkok, I spent hours just aimlessly wandering the streets and alleyways next to Inn a Day. It feels like a Bangkok time capsule over here.

★**Style:** Privates + Multi-Private Rooms
💸**Budget:** $$$
📍**Where:** Near Tha Tian Pier near Khao San Road

BOOK HERE

. . . .

FUN FACT!

Getting fake braces in Thailand is a niche trendy look.

Casa Nithra Hotel

Rooftop pool alert! You'll love that Casa Nithra is located near (but not on) Khao San Road so that you can get a deep night's sleep and then rise and shine for nearby sightseeing such as the Grand Palace and Reclining Buddha or wandering the famous Khao San Road. After a long day of walking under the Thai sun, coming back to get in the pool is such a treat.

★ **Style:** Privates
Budget: $$
Where: Khao San Road Area

BOOK HERE

PRO TIP! Try to book online days in advance, they book up quickly. If they're fully booked online, however, try just showing up. They usually have some rooms saved for walk-in customers.

••

Shanghai Mansion

You'll feel like a Bond girl staying in the Shanghai Mansion. This place screams Asian glamor with brightly painted walls, velvet lounge chairs, lanterns to set the mood, dark wooden canopy beds, and deep bathtubs that will make you want to strip down to everything but pearls. There is much to see, eat, and photograph in Chinatown and this hotel puts you smack dab in the center of it all. Not to mention, a free mini bar and walking tour. Get it, girl.

PRO TIP! Chinatown is located near Hua Lamphong Train Station and is just a quick taxi ride away from Khao San Road.

★ **Style:** Privates
Budget: $$
Where: Chinatown (Yaowarat)

BOOK HERE

••

Villa De Khaosan by Chillax

Party like a kid, hotel like an adult – Villa de Khaosan offers the best of both worlds, just a 10-minute walk from Khaosan Road. This location is ideal for sightseeing, temple hopping, shopping, and some partying, if you're in the mood.

Come back and lounge at the rooftop pool! I like this spot because it's close enough to the party life but far enough away that you won't be distrubed by any of the party noise at night. Plus, it's super affordable.

★ *Style:* Privates
Budget: $$
Where: Khao San Road

BOOK HERE

Mad Monkey Hostel

Staying near Khao San and want to party your face off? Mad Monkey is notorious for wild nights and lazy hangovers by the pool. Yes, I said pool! This dorm is pretty luxurious. The bar is massive, the beds are comfy and the food…hands down some of the best western food in Bangkok. The big plus to staying at Mad Monkey Hostel is that they've also got locations in Cambodia and The Philippines – so if your trip is headed that way, they can help sort you out. Also, if you're looking for a private room but still want social vibes – they've got really nice options with private bathrooms, as well.

★ *Style:* Dorms & Privates
Budget: $
Where: 55 Phra Sumen Rd
(Take a Taxi to Khao San Area/Phra Sumen Road)

BOOK HERE

Time Sabai 134

Finally, a non-party hostel. Time Sabai 134 feels like you're in Thailand with gorgeous ponds and trees and old-style Bangkok architecture…but with a modern twist. For half the noise and twice the space, stay next to Khao San Road instead of on it. Time Sabai 134 Hostel offers the most lux dorm beds. Traveling in pairs? You can also get a big dorm bed made for two people. Not to mention, the staff are so helpful in booking tours and giving travel advice.

★ *Style:* Dorms and Privates
Budget: $
Where: A 10-minute walk to Khao San Road

BOOK HERE

SUKHUMVIT AREA

Bangkok Marriott Hotel Sukhumvit

Hello, luxury. Hello, prime location. If you want to explore Sukhumvit the right way, stay at this super chic hotel that gives you access to all of Sukhumvit - from fancy bars to local life! The Marriott is world-famous for its rooftop skybar called Octave! Start your night with happy hour on the roof, then walk across the street to Soi 38 for my favorite street food spot in Sukhumvit! Then, head out for a night of live music and wine, then head back to your hotel, take a bath, slip into your robe and slippers then lounge in a bed that feels like floating clouds!

★ *Style:* Privates
Budget: $$$$
♥ *Where:* BTS Thong Lo

BOOK HERE

. . . .

Four Seasons Hotel Bangkok at Chao Phraya River

This is your chance to afford staying at a super luxury hotel without taking out a loan to pay for it! The Four Seasons Bangkok is one of the most affordable in the world! Here, your wish is your command with top tier service from the most accommodating hotel staff in town. The Four Seasons will arrange tours, hotel transport, room service, special requests, anything you want! Visit the spa, gym, rooftop, and certainly don't skip the bar where you can mingle with all sorts of interesting people from around the world.

The location is super interesting, right on the Chao Phraya River, between the Khao San Area and the Sukhumvit Area. The closest BTS stop is called Saphin Taksin, where you can hop on the water taxi that will take you to the Khao San Area, Bang Krachao and Wat Arun. You can also hop on the BTS and explore Sukhumvit.

★ *Style:* Privates
Budget: $$$$
♥ *Where:* Saphin Taksin

BOOK HERE

Bangkok Tree House

Glamping in Bang Krachao (the "Green Lung" I told you about earlier). Have you ever slept in a bird's nest with no walls, windows or ceiling? Have you ever woken up in the treetops overlooking the river? No? There's a first time for everything at The Bangkok Treehouse, an upscale eco-friendly bamboo resort located in the jungles of Bangkok. Surrounded by turtles, birds, fireflies, temples, and floating markets – get a taste of the real Thailand without leaving the city. Plus, as an eco-conscious hotel, The Bangkok Treehouse composts, hires locals within walking distance, and removes 1-kilo of trash from the river for every guest booked. Make an impact together.

★ *Style:* Private Tree House
Budget: $$$
♀ *Where:* On the River in Bang Krachao, you'll have to take a boat to get here - the hotel will help you arrange it!
Address: 60 Moo1 Soi Bua Phueng Pattana, Bang Namphueng

BOOK HERE

• •

The Yard

"A social hostel, but not a party hostel", the Yard is truly one of a kind. As the name suggests, there's a big grassy yard where you can lounge with a book or join in on some yoga. There's also a multimedia room to watch movies, a shabby chic bar on site for meeting other travelers, an amazing Burger restaurant out front, and the trendy Ari neighborhood to explore. With the BTS, the MoChit Bus + Train station and the popular Chatuchak Market nearby- this place is top choice for convenience if you want to explore Bangkok and then move on to other destinations in Thailand. Oh, and they have free bikes!

★ *Style:* Dorms + Multi-bed Privates for Sharing
Budget: $
♀ *Where:* Sukhumvit – Ari BTS – Walk towards Soi 51

BOOK HERE

Galleria 10

Social pool, prime location, trendy rooms and the best damn breakfast in the entire city of Bangkok- what more could a girl ask for? Perhaps a welcome coconut brought to you by a cute bellboy? Done. Galleria 10 will treat you like a queen, plus they've got a fabulous rooftop bar & pool with yummy food and fancy drink specials. With social events and parties throughout the week, this place is ideal for solo girl travelers...and where I usually stay when I come to Sukhumvit.

★**Style:** Privates
Budget: $$$
♥ **Where:** Sukhumvit- BTS Asok

BOOK HERE

. . . .

Victory Park Hostel

Stay here for Chatuchak Market, too!

It can be a struggle to find a private room at a budget price on Sukhumvit Road- but I've got one for you. Victory Park Hostel is a quaint guest house with clean, but simple rooms. Here, you've got a comfy bed, safe space, and friendly reception. Not to mention, the owner goes above and beyond to personal care for you... including making breakfast himself! Just steps from the BTS, massages, and the center of Bangkok - this a great choice when you want a little bit of privacy without spending above your budget.

★**Style:** Privates
Budget: $
♥ **Where:** Victory Monument

BOOK HERE

. . . .

♥ The girl who is reading this book now and the girl who will be sitting at a sky bar in Bangkok… are two different people. This trip will change you, whether you like it or not.

Best Tours in Bangkok

Bangkok is a big city. Even if you don't usually love tours, I highly recommend that you trust in a local guide to help you explore Bangkok beneath the surface!

 01 Bangkok Floating Market Tour with Pook

 05 Cooking Class and Market Tour

02 Free Bicycle Tour for Guests of Old Capital Bike Inn

06 Tuk Tuk Tour at Night, Including Markets, Temples and Food

 03 Bangkok Street Food Tour with Courageous Kitchen

 07 A Private Temple Tour to Help you Absorb all the History

04 See all the Bangkok Highlights in One Day

08 Chinatown Sights and Bites Tour

Must-See Sights in Bangkok

KHAO SAN ROAD AREA

Wat Traimit

I asked a local Bangkok boy to "show me something I've never seen before" and he took me to Wat Traimit, Bangkok's Temple of the Golden Buddha in Chinatown.

For years, since my first trip to Cambodia in 2014, I've heard tales of the most beautiful Giant Golden Buddha, glittering in precious gold, that had to be hidden from invading armies in the 13th century. The local craftsmen disguised the glittering buddha by covering it in gray, dull plaster.

The armies left none of the secret-keepers alive and so much time had passed, that the Golden Buddha was forgotten. So it was by accident, in 1955, that the Golden Buddha was discovered when it was being moved and was dropped, cracking the plaster and revealing the world's largest gold seated Buddha measuring nearly 3 meters tall and weighing nearly five and a half tons.

Located in Chinatown, Wat Traimit is just a 5-minute walk from Hua Lamphong Train station. Put it on your list before you take the train to Chiang Mai.

Budget: $.60 USD / 20 THB
Open: Daily 9am - 5pm
Where: Near Hua Lamphong Train Station
Address: 661 Charoen Krung Rd

Wat Po –Temple of the Reclining Buddha

This 46-meter long Buddha glistens in gold as it lounges on its side in a pose that is scarcely seen around the world. Just as impressive as the golden Buddha itself, are the monks' ceremonies that take place at Wat Po. Listen to the echoes of Sanskrit mantras as you wander the meticulously adorned temples with smaller Buddha statues galore. Purchase a bowl of gold coins where you can make a wish as you drop each coin into the 108 bronze bowls that line the temple- each drop ringing with an enchanting chime.

BONUS! Wat Po is also known as one of the best places to get a traditional Thai massage at their Thai school.

Budget: $3 USD / 100 THB
Open: Daily 8:00am – 5pm
Where: Maharat Road
Address: 2 Sanamchai Road, Grand Palace Sub District

The Grand Palace & Wat Prakeaw

What used to be the home of King Rama I and his harem, guarded by combat-trained female sentries, is now the most popular tourist attraction in Bangkok. Prepare to spend hours exploring this royal compound with over 100 golden buildings featuring over 200 years of royal and governmental history.

Head to the Outer Court where you'll find the main attraction- The Emerald Buddha (Wat Prakeaw). With French-inspired structures, ancient thrones and sparkling rooftops, the entire scene is captivating. Hire a guide inside the walls to get the full story.

🏷 **Budget:** $15 USD / 500 THB
🕗 **Open:** Daily 8:30am- 3:30pm
📍 **Where:** Khao San Area
🚇 **Address:** Na Phra Lan Road, Old City near Khao San Road

Wat Arun – The Temple of Dawn

My absolute favorite temple in all of Thailand lies just across the Chao Phraya River. Composed of dozens of intricate skyscraper temples adorned with white tiles, Wat Arun is unique to all other Buddhist temples in Thailand as it was built as an architectural representation of Mount Meru, or the center of the universe according to Buddhist cosmology. Keep an eye out for the statues of the guardian gods who stand at the 4 corners of the temple as protection.

PRO TIP! After you visit Wat Arun, order a Grab Taxi to take you to Wang Lang Market or exit the temple and walk 20 minutes to your left!

🏷 **Budget:** 100 Baht
🕗 **Open:** Daily 8:30am - 5:30 pm

↺ **How to Get There:** Across from Wat Pho in the Khao San Area, walk to Tha Tien Express Boat Pier. Tell them "Wat Arun" and you'll be directed toward the 3 baht river taxi to take you over.

Wat Saket – The Golden Mountain

For the most pristine views of Bangkok, you're going to want to head over to Wat Saket where you'll journey up a 300-step winding staircase to the top. Along the way, gong the drums and ring the bells that line your path. Once you reach the top, prepare for a breathtaking 360-degree view of the city.

BONUS! At the base of the temple, you'll find an ancient cemetery tracing back to the Ayutthaya period (1350- 1767 AD) covered in vines and mystery.

🏷 *Budget:* $.60 USD / 20 THB
⊙ *Open:* Daily 9am - 5pm
📍 *Where:* Near Khao San Road - Between Boriphat Road and Lan Luang Road, off Ratchadamnoen Klang Road
🚇 *Address:* 344 Khwaeng Ban Bat, Khet Pom Prap Sattru Phai

Pak Khlong Talat - The Flower Market

As you walk through the narrow stalls of Pak Khlong Talat, surrounded by rare orchids and bundles of roses, you'll need to step out of the way as men pulling carts of flowers and petals weave in and out of the market like they're in traffic. Stop to watch women weaving bright yellow marigold petals into offerings for temples and walk slowly as you take in the smells and sounds of more flowers than you've ever seen being prepared to be sent around the city the next morning.

BONUS! Walk around the neighborhood and you'll find some authentic Thai food stalls.

⊙ *Best Time to Go:* After 7pm
↺ *How to Get There:* Take a GrabCar or a 25-minute walk from Khao San

Amphawa Floating Market

There are 5 floating markets in Bangkok; Amphawa being my top pick for the perfect balance of humans to stalls. In other words, less crowded than others and more space for you to explore.

Wander over to the boardwalk and boat vendors will paddle over to you offering soups, grilled meat, coconuts, beverages and more right from their boat. You'll be given a tiny stool to enjoy your treats while you gaze out at the mesmerizing sights.

When you've had enough to eat, take an hour-long boat tour along the river, which stops to visit temples and a zany petting zoo; rent a bicycle to tour the town; shop til you drop with plenty of clothing and souvenir stalls; or stay until nightfall to go firefly watching on the river. All of these activities will be available to arrange once you show up to the market- just keep your eye out for ad signs.

PS. Boat tours are 50 baht per person in the public tour or 500 baht for a private tour.

🪁 **Budget:** Free
⊙ **Open:** Friday – Sunday 8:00am-7:00pm
📍 **Where:** Amphawa- 50 km from Bangkok

SUKHUMVIT AREA

The Green Lung of Bangkok

Easily, one of the best (and most surprising) days you'll have in Bangkok! You wouldn't expect to find rivers, jungles, and a national park in the big city...but that's exactly what this is!

The Green Lung is a massive peninsula just over the river from Sukhumvit that takes you back in time 30 years. The land is preserved, the locals have kept their customs, and the markets are as authentic as it gets.

Climb aboard the local ferry (5 baht) that zips you across the river for a day of exploring. Upon landing at the pier, you'll be greeted by bicycle vendors that will rent you a bike, give you a map, and send you on your way.On the map, you'll find these FREE adventures:

◊ Siamese Fighting Fish Gallery
◊ Sri Nakhon Khuean Khan Park and Botanical Garden
◊ Glittering Golden Temples like Wat Rat Rangsan, Wat Bang Kobua, and Wat Kong Kaew
◊ The Floating Market - Talad Nam Bang Nam Peung (only on the weekends)

You'll ride down small village roads between palm trees, flower fields, roadside food stands and wooden houses on stilts, passing other bicyclists and the occasional car – it's a very safe and slow journey.

You can easily ride for 4 hours or 1 hour – this road loops around for a customizable escapade.

PRO TIPS...
✔ Wear sunscreen
✔ Bring small bills for local vendors
✔ Start early – around 9am for the best weather
✔ Bring a shawl or wear something that covers your shoulders for the temples
✔ Stay at Bangkok Tree House Eco Hotel for a fully-immersed getaway

♻ *How to Get There:*
○ *Option 1:* Go to BTS Khlong Toei and take a taxi to Klong Toey pier. Here you can take a longtail boat (100 baht) or a water taxi (10 baht) across.

○ *Option 2:* Go to BTS Bang Na and take a taxi (5 baht) to Wat Bangna Nok Pier. Get on the water taxi that takes you directly to the gorgeous Wat Bang Nam Phueng Nok – so easy.

PRO TIP! Option 2 is cheaper, more local and drops you in the center of all the attractions. Go left for the floating market and go right for the park and fighting fish.

Visit Erawan Shrine
While you're out and about for a day of shopping near Siam center, take a moment to find peace at the Erawan Shrine. Unlike most shrines in Bangkok, this one isn't Buddhist. This is a Hindu temple featuring the Thai representation of Brahma, the Hindu god of creation. One of the most beautiful shrines in Bangkok with glittering gold statues and fresh flowers placed by gracious followers everyday.

⊙ **Open:** Daily 6:00am-11:00pm
♻ *How to Get There:* BTS Chit Lom (Chidlom)- Exit 1

Soi Cowboy

Soi Cowboy is certainly not everyone's cup of tea- but for some, it's totally fascinating. I'll leave the morality debate out of this one and let you decide where you stand. But if you're curious, read on.

Bangkok's most popular Red-Light street is wild with women and ladyboys who line the street in scantily clad outfits, pulling men into their clubs to watch the girls dance (usually with their tops on) and have a drink.
The neon lights and loud music usually kick off around 9pm, and if you're not easily shocked, it can be quite a "cultural" experience to pop into one of the clubs for a drink. The drinks serve as your cover charge (usually 100-175 baht each).

You'd think that this street would feel super sketchy and unsafe- but it doesn't. The girls are nice, the street is brightly lit, and there are tourists from all over the world hanging out to watch the madness. And when you've had enough, the safe haven of Terminal 21 Shopping Center is just across the street (3-minute walk).

❂*How to Get There:* MRT Sukhumvit Station or BTS Asok. Located 100 meters from Terminal 21- between Asok Road and Soi 23

SAFE GIRL TIP

As my mother used to say, "nothing good can happen after midnight". It's not the men that you have to worry about- they'll be too distracted by the persistent bar girls and will leave you alone. Rather, this is the time of night where pickpockets see a window of opportunity.
Keep your purse close.

Shopping in Bangkok

KHAO SAN ROAD AREA

Khao San Road and Rambuttri Road

It's time to learn the art of haggling on Khao San. The vendor says 200 baht for those elephant pants? Nah, you can get them for 150 if you're confident. Find anything you want on Khao San from gorgeous dresses and handmade jewelry to tailored suits and fake IDs. Keep your eye out for Suzy Walking Street, which is a cut-through alley between Khao San and Soi Rambuttri that offers hippie-esque jewelry, art and tattoo shops.

☉ **Open:** Stalls open up roughly around 9am and stay open past midnight
↻ **How to Get There:** From Sukhumvit, take the BTS to National Stadium and then hop in a taxi.

SUKHUMVIT AREA

Siam

This cosmopolitan shopping area has your favorite retailers from home like Forever21, H&M, & Uniqlo alongside the upscale Siam Paragon that boasts Armani, Chanel, and Dior. Spend a day in air-conditioning with a movie at the Paragon Cineplex or some fun at the musical bowling alley. Paragon has a great food court and gourmet grocery store in case you get hungry.

☉ **Open:** Daily 10am–10pm
↻ **How to Get There:** BTS Siam/Chit Loem

Terminal 21 Shopping Center

Mimicking an international airport, each floor of Terminal 21 is themed like a different city around the world. Paris has a MAC store and H&M, Tokyo and

London have tons of Thai clothing boutiques, Istanbul has a NYX makeup store, and San Francisco is home to the most amazing food court around—seriously... best food court in the city. Get out of the heat for the day with a movie on the top floor, Los Angeles.

○ **Open:** Daily 10am–10pm
↻ **How to Get There:** BTS Asok

MBK Center

Within this massive mall stacked with floor after floor of electronics, gadgets, clothing, and more—there is one floor that stands out from the rest!

When you've lost, broken or had your phone stolen, head to phone heaven on the 4th floor of MBK. 1st hand and 2nd hand phones are displayed in case after case—it's just a matter of finding a vendor you want to work with. Get a replacement or a Chinese off-brand phone that is just as good and twice as cheap. You can also get your phones and tablets repaired here!

Afterwards, check out the clothing floor, the furniture floor, the camera floor and so on. Once you've worked up an appetite, head outside to the food market and get your grub on!

○ **Open:** Daily 10am–10pm
↻ **How to Get There:** BTS National Stadium

DID YOU KNOW? There are over 35,000 Buddhist Temples in Thailand

Street Food & Markets in Bangkok

NOT-SO-FUN FACT: The Bangkok government has pledged to "ban" street food in Bangkok despite the city being internationally ranked for the best street food in the world. They aren't really living up to that "ban" but it does mean you'll need a little extra help in finding the best street food. Don't worry- I know the best kept street secrets in BKK and will help you find them.

Take a Food Tour with the Foodie King of Bangkok:

Dwight! Look for his Airbnb Experience Tour:

Street Food 101 in Local Bangkok

Soi 38

Don't let anyone tell you that Soi 38 street food doesn't exist anymore—it does. The street food has just gone underground. Walk onto Soi 38 anytime after 5pm and you'll find an old parking garage converted into a food hawkers site with tons of stands, stalls, and places to sit! Tastes dishes from the north, south, and central regions. They've also got Chinese, Japanese, and hotpot! Plenty of vegetarian options, too.

My absolute favorite bowl of soup in the city is located in Soi 38 (I literally dream about this soup). The first stall on the right, under the roof, is called Mill. Order their vegetarian spicy noodle soup and prepare to fall in love.

⊘ *Best Time:* Sun–Mon 5pm–10pm
♀ *Where:* Near BTS Thonglor, Road 38

Things to try:

♥ Mango Sticky Rice   ♥ Crab Fried Rice   ♥ Massaman Chicken Curry

Wang Lang Market

The only true flea market in Bangkok, Wang Lang Market is an off the beaten tourist path' gem. Everything from handmade leather wallets to an infinite supply of shoes- this is a bargain shopper's paradise. Of course, what would a Thai market be without food? Get your fill of curry, sushi, bubble tea and those cute little artsy desserts for beyond reasonable prices.

☉ **Open:** Daily 10am to sunset

♥ **Where:** Near Khao San and Wat Arun

↺ **How to Get There:** Take a water taxi (across from the Grand Palace in the Khao San Area) and get off at Prannok Pier (Wanglong N10)

Chatuchak Market

Clear your schedule for the day, lather on the sunscreen, and prepare to shop til you drop! Chatuchak Weekend Market is the biggest outdoor shopping market that you ever did see. Handmade purses, vintage records, essential oil infused soaps, souvenirs in bulk- you're about to hit the jackpot.

This market is divided into sections- some with clothing, some with high-end & handmade leather bags, some with furniture, some with animals…anything and everything you could want can be found at Chatuchak.

PRO TIP! If you see something you like and think, "Oh, I'll come back for it later"- you won't. You're going to get lost in the winding corridors of stalls and restaurants, but if you shop with a 'life is short' attitude, and just buy the damn thing, you'll have no regrets later.

☉ **Open:** Friday 6:00pm-Midnight/Saturday & Sunday 9:00am - 6:00pm

♥ **Where:** Near Sukhumvit

↺ **How to Get There:** Take BTS Mo Chit (Exit 1) or MRT Kamphaeng Phet (Exit 2) - and follow the crowds. Or just take a taxi directly

PRO TIP 2! Getting off at MRT Chatuchak is actually a super inconvenient walk!

Maeklong Railway "Folding Umbrella" Market (Talad Rom Hub)

📷 WILFRIED STRANG

Yes, the Folding Umbrella Market is technically a market– but really, coming here is more of a food/culture/history adventure than a shopping venture.

There's a market 80k on the outskirts of Bangkok where vendors sell their goods at the side of the train tracks to be closer to their customers. When the trains come through, the vendors scramble to close their umbrellas and scoot their goods (and themselves) clear of the train as it passes by, inches from their face.

For a true traveler's adventure, take the entire day to train hop your way to the market. Start at Wongwian Yai Railway Station and catch the train heading to Mahachai Station. Next, you'll take the ferry across Maeklong River – which will drop you off on the other side, Tha Chalom. Then, catch the train from Ban Laem Station to Maeklong. You have arrived.

In a hurry? Hire a taxi for around 1,000 baht for the 1.5 hour drive.

Don't want to go alone? Here's a tour that includes the Train Market and Amphawa Floating Market.

⊙ **Open:** 6 a.m. to 6 p.m
⊙ **Train Schedule:** 6:20 am, 8:30 am, 9 am, 11:10 am, 11:30 am, 2:30 pm, 3:30 pm, and 5:40 pm.

Khao San Road

Hangovers are best cured with Khao San street food starting in the AM. Smoothie stands with fresh fruit, soups that speak to your soul, and in my opinion- the best Pad Thai in Bangkok. And the morning street food rush is only the beginning. As night falls, vendors bring their carts round to offer wild and wonderful fare that goes perfectly with a cold walking beer.

⊖**Best Time:** All day – every day
♥ **Where:** Khao San Road & Rambutri Street

Things to try...

♥ Scorpion on a stick   ♥ Fried egg rolls

♥ Kebabs   ♥ Stewed Pork Leg over rice (Khao Kha Moo)

Srinagarindra Train Night Market

Guys, it's about to get real. Come hungry because the street food at this trendy Thai market never ends. Rows and rows of seafood, Thai salads, bite sized snacks, sushi and ice-cold walking beers await. Each section of the market offers a different niche. When you've had your fill, there are live music bars stacked in old shipping containers that surround the market. Sit down, order a bucket of beers on ice, bring your snacks, and soak up the best people watching.

This market is so big that it is divided into zones. The Warehouse Zone offers a collection of old electronics, Japanese memorabilia, vintage car collections, and more whacky finds. And the Market Zone has over 2000 stalls for buying modern clothes mixed with hippie everything. It's the biggest market with the most to eat, see, and buy, yet is relatively untouched by the backpacker community with its off-the-beaten-path location.

Things to try...

♥ Vintage Soda (look for a VW van)   ♥ Thai Fried Chicken Wings

♥ Kao Moek Gai (Muslim Rice and Chicken)   ♥ Mini Cupcakes

♥ Banana Roti   ♥ Seafood in a Bag (you get to eat with plastic gloves!)

♥ Beef Kebab

⊙**Best Time:** Thursday-Sunday 5pm to 12am

☾**How to Get There:** BTS On Nut is the closest station but requires a taxi journey from there.

♥ **Where:** Srinakarin Road Soi 51 - behind Seacon Square Mall

Sutthisan Market (Off-The-Beaten Path!)

To feed the two towers of Insurance Company workers, this market offers traditional Thai dishes morning, noon and night. In the morning, you'll find coffee stands, boat noodles and fresh fruit vendors. The afternoon has the best Khao Man Gai and lots of "point and pick" curry pots. In the evening, take the chance to try the best Tom Yum Soup you'll ever have in your life. It is located at a small Isaan (Northern Thai) restaurant just next to the bridge stairs by the MRT Exit 3. The Sunday Evening Market offers whole chicken, grilled shrimp, lots of curry, and even…fried bugs.

⊙**Open:** Daily 8am-1pm & 5pm-9pm

☾**How to Get There:** MRT Sutthisan

W District

Imagine an American Food Truck Park. You've got a dozen food stalls lining the perimeter of the space with tables and chairs in the center – fueled by one bar with a plethora of beer on tap. That's exactly what you'll find at W District near Phra Khanong BTS. The food stalls offer international options like Mexican, Indian and Italian. The bar offers Thai beers and imports. The clientele is mostly western expats living in Bangkok, so expect the prices to be a bit higher. Here you can get a big bottle of Singha Beer for 120 baht, whereas it's 100 baht on Khao San Road.

⊙**Best Time:** 4pm-12am

☾**How to Get There:** BTS Phra Khanong - Exit 3 – walk straight and turn left on Sukhumvit 69-71 and another left on Edison Alley

♥ **Where:** Sukhumvit 69-71 Phra Khanong

Where to Eat in Bangkok

...besides all those amazing markets I just listed, here are some other places you'll definitely want to eat.

KHAO SAN ROAD AREA

Khao Man Gai Stand

Khao Man Gai is my favorite Thai food dish to eat for breakfast. It's simple. It's chicken, fried or boiled, with rice steamed in the chicken broth and chicken broth on the side and served with the best damn spicy sauce on earth. They utilize the whole chicken to create this incredible dish! Come to this food stall for breakfast, order half crispy and half regular chicken. Important: order without the congealed blood cake (yep that's a thing) by saying "Mai ow luh-d".

On your way to sit down, you can grab a plastic cup and scoop up some water out of the water cooler (this is a classic bonus to Khao Man Gai stands). Sit down next to taxi drivers and police officers eating before they head to you. Your food will be brought to your table. Don't take a bite without your spicy sauce!

Watch my Bangkok Instagram highlight to see how I do it.

⊙ **Best Time:** Outside KC Guesthouse
⊙ **When:** Breakfast to lunch - when it's gone it's gone the earlier the better.

BONUS! There is a fantastic Khao Man Gai stand at night outside of Casa Nithra Hotel - I lived off of this stand during quarantine!

I Love Thai Food

The best Thai food for the best prices! You will eat here once a day every day you're on Khao San and the staff will likely remember what you like to drink after day 2. The Khao Soi is a must-order! They also have Tiger beer! Order it ice cold. Ps. Look for my stickers here and send me a photo!

⊙ **Open:** Daily lunch to late dinner
♀ **Where:** The very beginning of Rambuttri Rd. on the left.
🏛 **Address:** 128 Chakrabongse Rd

Maze Dining

High-end dishes by a chef from Chiang Mai, Maze Dining has caught the eye of Netflix

T&K Seafood

Chinatown is the place to be for fantastic seafood at backpacker prices. This place is hard to miss with their sprawling row of charcoal grills slowly cooking whole salted fish and juicy prawns. You'll notice the staff in bright green shirts, hustling hard to cater to every table. They've got an English menu with pictures so you can order to your heart's desire. Remember: it's Chinatown so plan to share! If you come alone, just order one main dish with a side of morning glory.

🕐 **Open:** Daily 4:30PM–2AM
↻ **How to Get There:** Take a taxi to Chinatown (Yaowarat)
🏠 **Address:** 49-51 Soi Phadung Dao, Yaowarat Rd, Bangkok (corner of Yaowarat Road and Soi Phadung Dao)

FUN FACT! If you want to take a deep dive into the Bangkok food scene, YouTube a guy named Mark Wiens- the foodie king of Thailand.

Everything in Chinatown

Chinatown is lined with food stalls. It's easy to peek at something, point to it, and pay for it (you need cash). Take your treat and eat while you walk and watch the street hawkers.

🕐 **Best Time:** Once the sun goes down and the area lights up!
↻ **How to Get There:** From Khao San Road, take a GrabTaxi or make a day of walking here - just know that it's a 30-minute walk which is best done when the sun starts to set.

Overrated Places to Skip

✗ Thip Samai Pad Thai

✗ Jay Fai Michelin Star Street Food

SUKHUMVIT AREA

Im Chan

"Eat where the locals eat" is always a good motto to live by while traveling. Im Chan serves the lunch rush full of Thai office personnel and shop workers who want traditional Thai food fast. With a menu full of pictures and English to go with them- you can eat just like the locals. Food is cheap, dishes are made to order, and location is central- what more could you ask for?

🕐 **Open:** 7am-10pm
↻ **How to Get There:** Phrom Phong BTS
🏠 **Address:** Sukhumvit 37 Alley

Tamnak Isan

Want to try true northern Thai food from the Isan region of Thailand. You won't find a Thai restaurant like this back home, so toss out your expectations for Pad Thai and Green Curry. Here, it's all about grilled meat, sticky rice, and cold beer. Here are some things to order, just remember to specify how spicy you like your food:

- ♥ Khao Newo (Sticky Rice)
- ♥ Grilled Fish (A big ass white fish served whole)
- ♥ Morning Glory (Sauteed Greens)
- ♥ Som Tam (Green Mango Salad)
- ♥ Pork Larb (A minced pork dish)
- ♥ BBQ Pork Neck Spicy Salad (the most tender pork ever)
- ♥ Grilled Chicken

If you want to try something SUPER local, order the Sweet Veggies with Ant Eggs. My neighbors in Chiang Mai love that shit.

⊙ **Open:** 11am – 11pm
↻ **How to Get There:** BTS Ekkamai- 10-minute walk down Soi 63
🚇 **Address:** 86/1 Sukhumvit 63 | Ekamai 8

Na Na se Ramen

Collagen chicken ramen with chicken meatballs. This is one of those bowls of soup that you eat once and think about for years...except, I ate here like once or twice a week when I lived in this neighborhood. Na Na se Ramen boils their ramen broth from scratch, extracting all the collagen (which is so good for you, by the way) that it creates a thick and creamy soup like I've never had before in my life.

⊙ **Open:** Daily 11am-midnight
↻ **How to Get There:** On Nut BTS
🚇 **Address:** Sukhumvit 79 Alley, Phra Khanong Nuea

Terminal 21 Food Court

Back home when you hear the term "food court" you think of subpar Chinese joints and fast food. Not in Thailand. Here's how it works: got to the top floor of Terminal 21 shopping mall, stand in line where you'll exchange cash for a prepaid food card, and then go crazy. They have some of the best street food options like Khao Man Gai, Stewed Pork Leg, and Mango Sticky rice. Best of all, it's all cooked in such a clean (and air conditioned) environment. When you're done, take your card back to the counter to retrieve what you didn't spend.

⊙ **Open:** Daily 10am–10pm

↻ **How to Get There:** Asok BTS, Terminal 21 Shopping Center, 5th floor

PRO TIP! Don't show up during the 12–1pm lunch rush and expect to find a seat.

Any Food Court in Bangkok

Don't stop with Terminal 21 Food Court. Bangkok (and Thailand) is filled with lunch-worthy food courts, each one a bit different than the next.

While Terminal 21 offers the most authentic Thai street food, other food courts have their own appeal. Many offer the most popular Taiwanese Bubble Tea Chains, Japanese Sushi, famous hot-pot, and lots of food from home like Subway, Dairy Queen and Cold Stone Creamery. Do yourself a favor and check out some of my favorite Bangkok food courts for lunch.

♥ **EmQuartier** – BTS Phrom Phong

♥ **Siam Paragon** – BTS Siam

♥ **MBK Center** – BTS National Stadium

♥ **Fortune Town** – MRT Rama 9

♥ **Big C Basement Food Court** - BTS Bearing

Phed Mark

One of the most respected food vloggers in the world is a guy named Mark who is based in Thailand, married to a Thai girl, speaks fluent Thai and is the king of finding the best Thai food in the entire country! It is only fitting that this Thai Food Guru opened his own Thai street food restaurant in Bangkok. But beware, his tagline is "If it's not spicy, I'm not eating" so be sure to tell your server just how much spice you can handle!

Check out Mark's channelhere and get some food inspiration!

⊙ **Open:** Monday-Saturday 10am-8pm

↻ **How to Get There:** Located directly in front of the Ekkamai Bus Terminal. Walk 1 minute from. Take exit 3 from Ekkamai BTS Station, go down the steps, make a u-turn, walk past the 7-11, and across the street.

🏛 **Address:** 928 Sukhumvit Rd, Khwaeng Phra Khanong, Khet Khlong Toei

📷 **PHEDMARK.COM**

Cabbages and Condoms

"Our food won't make you pregnant." Yep, that's the actual slogan of C&C. If you want to make a difference while in Thailand and keep others like you from getting pregnant, support a restaurant with a cause. C&C contributes revenue towards family planning services in Thailand. A little contradictory however—the atmosphere here is quite romantic with twinkling lights dangling from lush trees in an intimate garden. Maybe that's why they send you home with condoms.

- ⊙ **Open:** Daily 11am–10pm
- ↻ **How to Get There:** Asok BTS, Exit 2
- ⛩ **Address:** Sukhumvit 12 Alley, Khwaeng Khlong Toe

Soei

Want to try real real Thai food? Let the man himself, P'Soei, cook for you. Dishes like Goong Chae Nam Pla (sort of like Wasabi shrimp ceviche) and Yam Kai Dao (Thai fried egg salad) will change everything you thought you knew about Thai food. This is certainly a must-try spot for anyone that has a foodie soul. The feel of the restaurant is very personal as P'Soei has photos from his days of playing Rugby all around the restaurant and even a couple photos of that time the famous foodie, Andrew Zimmern, stopped by.

- ⊙**Open:** Daily 10 am – 9:30 pm (Closed on Saturday)
- ↻**How to Get There:** Sanam Pao BTS – then hop in a taxi
- ⛩ **Address:** Near the corner of Phibun Whattana Yaek 6 and Rama VI Soi 34. Moo Baan Piboon Wattana neighborhood (you can find this place on Google Maps).

Best Beef

Imagine this: fresh plates of prawns, sliced beef, pork tenderloin, garlic bread, veggies, and more brought to you to cook at your table on a charcoal grill as you order. Sounds pretty good, right? What if I told you that this was an all-you-can-eat situation spanning 2-hours for 269baht? And then, what if I told you that for 439 baht, you could get 2-hours of all-you-can-eat AND all-you-can-drink beer and cocktails. You're sold, aren't you?

- ⊙ **Open:** Daily 4pm-12am
- ↻ **How to Get There:** On Nut BTS – go straight out of Exit 2, walk for 5 minutes and look for the huge sign
- ⛩ **Address:** 1490/2 Sukhumvit Rd, Khlong Tan

Bars in Bangkok

Honestly, my favorite bar in Thailand is 7 Eleven. I'm a big fan of grabbing a beer and sitting on a curb outside people watching. But when you want to class it up, here you go…

KHAO SAN AREA
Poh Tha Tien

I found this absolute gem of a bar on accident and it still feels like my little secret. Poh Tha Tien is hidden in plain sight, up a flight or stairs inside The Tien Pier! Walk into the pier towards the water and take a right with the water on your left. Welcome to my secret club house where you drink cold beer, eat free peanuts and watch the sunset over Wat Arun. You can also order food here but really, you're coming for the ambiance, beers, and cute ladies that laugh at you when you try to speak Thai.

☉ **Open:** 6pm-midnight
♥ **Where:** Inside Tha Tien Pier

Ku Bar

The most truly hidden bar in all of Bangkok is Ku Bar. Look this place up on GoogleMaps and it looks like an abandoned hospital after an apocalypse. It's not creepy or dangerous, though, it's just a very well-kept secret.

↻ **How to Get There:** Walk down the alley next to Brown Sugar Jazz Bar (which is closed but still on GoogleMaps) until you find a wooden door that looks like someone's front door. Walk up to the 3rd floor. You'll be in a semi-empty building and start feeling lost right about now. Keep going. Follow the arrows on the wall until you see a wood-paneled sliding door and viola! Friendly (non-serial-killer) hosts will be waiting to warmly greet you with a small menu of incredible cocktails! Head downstairs inside the bar for a terrific wine list at their wine bar.

Ps. I know this sounds super dangerous for a solo girl but you'll be okay doing this one alone. I recommend going on GoogleMaps before you go so you can see photos of what to expect.

🕑 **Open:** Wed-Sun 6pm to midnight
📍 **Where:** Old Town, a 12-minute walk from Khao San Road
🏛 **Address:** 469 Phra Sumen Rd

Teens of Thailand

The only gin bar in Thailand, TOT is for you girls who appreciate a fine, hand-crafted cocktail made with gourmet ingredients by some Thai dudes who know what they are doing! This intimate speakeasy is filled with hip vibes and a laidback creative Thais. TOT is near Hua Lamphong Train Station and is a perfect stop off before a night train journey.

🕑 **Open:** Daily 7pm–1am
↻ **How to Get There:** Take a taxi to Soi Nana in Chinatown or take the MRT to Hua Lamphong and take a 5 minute walk
🏛 **Address:** 76 Khwaeng Pom Prap, Khet Pom Prap Sattru Phai

PS. TOT isn't closed, their entrance is just super low-key. Push those wooden doors open.

NOTE: Oh man, this place was just featured on a Netflix show which means it's going to get crowded. Usually I take places off my list once they get to be famous, but this one stays!

Hey! Anyone who doesn't support you taking this trip doubts their own abilities to travel, not yours.

Don't let their fear dictate your life.

SUKHUMVIT AREA

Craft

Tacos, burgers, and craft beer in backyard BBQ kind of setting with twinkly lights and a warm summer breeze. Yes. Craft is where you need to be when the sun starts to set and your tummy starts to rumble. First, order yourself a juicy burger and fries, then get to the beer menu. With 40 beers on tap and tons of craft bottles, Craft is the most extensive craft beer bar in the city. That first sip of craft beer from home after weeks of sipping Singha might just bring a tear to your eye. And on Friday nights you can catch some live music—usually along the tunes of acoustic folk and blues.

- ⊙ **Open:** 12pm–10pm
- ↻ **How to Get There:** BTS Asok, Exit 4. 10 minute walk.
- 🛏 **Address:** 16 Soi Sukhumvit 23 Khwaeng Khlong Toei

Havana Social

If you want cigars, mojitos, and empanadas, I can tell you where to go. But first, you'll need to find the telephone booth on Soi 11 which serves to "recreate the Pre-Revolutionary era of Cuba" when each speakeasy was hidden. Sometimes you need to punch a passcode into the phone to get in (which can be found on Havana Social's FB page and other times a bouncer will sneak you in). Friday & Saturday at 10pm is the best time to go for social vibes and live music.

- ⊙ **Open:** Daily 6pm–2am
- ↻ **How to Get There:** BTS Nana, Exit 2. Look for the little alley in front of Fraser Suites
- 🛏 **Address:** Sukhumvit Soi 11

 SKYBARSIN BANGKOK

Octave

'Holy shit' is the only way to describe Bangkok's #1 sky bar—Octave. The 360° view of BKK's city skyline, the playful EDM beats, the breezy sunset—it all feels so surreal and euphoric at the same time. Happy Hour is everyday from 5–7pm with killer cocktails for 220 Baht. You can easily snag a table if you show up at 5pm but reserving a table ahead of time is a smart move, too. FYI: there is a dress code. Come looking polished instead of wearing your elephant pants.

⊙ **Open:** Daily 5pm–2am
⊙ **Happy Hour:** Daily 5–7pm
↻ **How to Get There:** Thong Lor BTS, Exit 3, Rooftop of the Marriot Hotel
🚉 **Address:** 57 Sukhumvit Rd, Klongtan-Nua

Tichuca Rooftop Bar

Right across from Octave is Tichuca - is Bangkok's newest sky bar and one of the most dramatic! The architecture is insane...which has made this place the new Instagram spot. You've been warned. If you want to sit at the Instagram Bar, message them first and make a reservation: +66 65 878 5562

⊙ **Open:** Daily 6pm-midnight
↻ **How to Get There:** ThongLor BTS
🚉 **Address:** T-One Building 8, 46th Floor

Brewski

Brewski is a laidback rooftop bar with beautiful views and beautiful brews. You can get a variety of craft beers on tap for around 300 Baht. They serve you a fancy bowl of peanuts to munch on while you peruse their tapas menu. Everyday they offer a 'Pint of the Day' happy hour and along with rotating food specials like Taco Tuesday and Pulled Pork Thursday. Brewski doesn't get too crowded so you can rock up and find a seat with no problem. There are a few large tables for big groups and some intimate spaces that offer a bit more of a romantic experience.

- 🕐 *Open:* Daily 5pm–1am
- 🕐 *Happy Hour:* Daily 5–8pm
- ♻ *How to Get There:* BTS Asok, Exit 4, Rooftop of the Radisson Blu 30ᵗʰ floor
- 🚇 *Address:* 489 Sukhumvit Rd Tan

Above Eleven

Salsa Ladies Night on Wednesdays, Live Jazz on Thursdays, and a live DJ every night in-between—Above Eleven knows how to throw a good party. The cherry on top is the 360° view of BKK's glittering skyline where you can get cozy on comfy couches while enjoying an incredible Japanese Peruvian Fusion menu and signature cocktails. The semi-casual dress code is an excuse to get dressed up—who doesn't love that?

- 🕐 *Open:* Daily 6pm–2am
- 🕐 *Happy Hour:* Daily 6pm–10pm
- ♻ *How to Get There:* BTS Nana, Rooftop of the Frasier Sweets
- 🚇 *Address:* 38/8 Soi Sukhumvit 11

Vanilla Sky

Lately, my go-to rooftop bar is Vanilla Sky, located on the 36ᵗʰ floor of the Sky Compass Hotel on Sukhumvit. It's breezy, spacious and modern with gorgeous, panoramic views of the glittering city. The drinks are beautiful, the music is catchy and best of all…Vanilla Sky is never full! This means no lines and no waiting for 15 minutes just to get a drink! The dress-code is smart casual, so no flip flops or swimsuits!

- 🕐 *Open:* Daily 5pm–1:30am

 Hey, do you follow my travel avdentures on Instagram yet?
xoxo, Alexa

More Things to Do in Bangkok

The #1 Things is markets - if you spent your whole trip just market-hopping, I'd be proud of you. But I know you want to mix it up so here's more gems that are worth your precious time.

Get A Thai Massage

While you can consider Thai Massage as a form of relaxation, it's actually a centuries old spiritual practice. You'll be bent like a pretzel, squeezed like a lemon and walked on like a pretty little doormat—but it feels so good in the end. Thai massage releases toxins from your body and leaves you feeling like a new, more flexible, woman. No oils here, in fact, you'll be provided clothing to wear during the process.

♀ Where: You'll see Thai massage parlors everywhere!
Budget: around $6-9 USD/200 Baht per hour

Bangkok Forensic Medicine Museum

Bangkok Forensic Medicine Museum, also known as Siriraj Medical Museum, is made up of 4 museum in one, exhibiting the bizarre side of nature, medicine, and death. Get up close and personal with diseased specimen, common parasites, dissected human organs, real-life embalmed bodies of the deceased, and even a mummified cannibal who loved to eat children. Oh, Thailand.

⊘ Open: Mon–Sat 9am–4pm
Price: $1.20 USD/40 Baht
↻ How to Get There: Take the water taxi to Prannok Pier
Address: 2 Wanglung Rd Khwaeng Siriraj, Khet Bangkok No

Watch a Muay Thai Boxing Match

Thai Boxing is a national treasure all across Thailand. From the ceremonious music to the gambling crowds to the high paced action in the ring- it's an all-around exhilarating experience. Don't be alarmed when you see kids in the ring- they've been well trained and can hold their own. You can buy tickets from your hotel in advance or jump in a taxi and have them drop you off. There are 3 big stadiums in Bangkok...

📷 BRADY WEEKS PHOTOGRAPHY

❶ Rajadamnern Boxing Stadium:

Built in 1945, this is a classic Muay Thai stadium with lots of locals!

🕐 *Fight Times:* Monday, Wednesday, Thursday & Sunday starting at 6:00pm
💸 *Budget:* Starts at $30 USD / 1000 baht
📍 *Where:* Just north of Khao San
🚕 *Address:* 1 Ratchadamnoen Nok Rd, Pom Prap, Khet Pom Prap Sattru Phai, Krung Thep Maha Nakhon 10200

Book VIP Tickets for $60 USD/ 2000 baht here ☞

❷ Lumpinee Boxing Stadium

The most popular with tourist companies and easy to access via the BTS + Taxi

⊙ *Fight Times:* Tuesday-Friday fight at 18:30 & Saturday fights at 4:00pm & 8:00pm

Budget: Starts at $30 USD / 1000 baht

♥ *Where:* Just north of BTS Mo Chit

Address: No.6, Ramintra Rd, Anusawaree

Book VIP Tickets for $60 USD/ 2000 baht here ☞

❸ Channel 7 Stadium

Located off the Mo Chit BTS. Broadcast live on Channel 7, this place gets packed with locals so arrive an hour before to get a seat. Also, for TV purposes... wear black.

⊙ *Fight Times:* Sunday 12:45pm

Budget: Free!

♥ *Where:* Just north of BTS Mo Chit

Address: 998/1 Chom Phon, Chatuchak

Take a Muay Thai Boxing Class

Might as well learn to kick ass while in Thailand. While you can drop in to any Muay Thai gym for a class, the most traveler-friendly Muay Thai gym is Master Toddy's. They offer tailored classes for total beginners where you will learn the basics of Muay Thai including how to spar, kick, and throw a few trick moves against the Thai master.

⊙ *Class Time:* Mon–Fri 7:30am–9:30am & 4pm–6pm, Sat 7:30am–9:30am

↻ *How to Get There:* Take a taxi from BTS Bearing

Address: 55/103–109 Sukhumvit 107, Bearing Soi 22

Go on a Bicycle Tour

Some of the best Bangkok adventures are not available by foot. After all, this city is massive. But on two wheels, you can access off-the-beaten path temples, small-town neighborhoods, and rural pockets of the city that would otherwise be unreachable.

Link up with the amazing crew at 'Follow Me Bike Tour' for an unforgettable local experience. There are tons of bike tours to choose from including jungle tours, street food tours, night tours and more. Tours range from 4–8 hours with entertaining guides and all gear provided.

⊙ **Open:** Daily! Times depend on the tour!

💵 **Budget:** $40 USD/1,300 Baht per person

📍 **Where:** Sathorn Soi 9, 126 (33/6)

🌐 **Visit:** followmebiketour.com

Bangkok Comedy Club

See a different side of Bangkok culture as you join expats living in Bangkok and travelers from around the globe for a night of humor and beer at the Comedy Club. The comedy club invites world-class comedians to debut improv and stand up bits that never disappoint. Afterwards, the whole club gathers downstairs at The Royal Oak Restaurant and Bar with good vibes and great cocktails.

💵 **Budget:** Starting at $12 US / 400 baht

🔄 **How to Get There:** Phrom Phong BTS – head towards Soi 33/1 and look for Royal Oak Restaurant (the club is upstairs)

🏛 **Address:** 595/10 Sukhumvit Soi 33/1

Cooking with Poo and Friends

"Oh, here's just a little something I learned how to whip up while in Thailand". This cooking class is great for anyone with just a few days to spend in Bangkok! They'll pick you up at the conveniently located meeting point Emporium Sweets next to BTS Prom Pong at 8:30am, where you'll be whisked away with your Thai chefs to shop in the local morning market to buy all of the ingredients you'll be cooking with that day. You'll learn how to prepare a 4 course Thai meal and then…you get to eat it. Win-win. Book ahead via their website.

⊙ **Open:** Daily 8:30am–1pm

Massages & Spas in Bangkok

Sabaijai Thai Massage

Just my go-to Thai massage spot on Khao San Road. The women are licensed and absolute experts. I recommend you try a different massage each time you come. Get a classic Thai massage, a foot massage and a head, neck and shoulder massage. They are each hypnotic in their own way. You'll love the massage and you'll also love the prices!

⊙ **Open:** Daily 10am – 10pm
♥ **Where:** 12-minute walk from Khao San Road in Old Town

Find it on GoogleMaps!

Perception Blind Massage

Blind and visually impaired massage therapists offer relaxing foot massages, Thai massages and aromatherapy oil massage with professional treatment. While prices are 200–300 Baht more expensive here than other massage shops, the money helps support a community of people who are healing themselves by healing others. The atmosphere is clean, calm and modern—you'll feel relaxed the second you walk in the door.

⊙ **Open:** 10am–10pm
↻ **How to Get There:** BTS Chongnonsee Exit 2, Silom Area
🚉 **Address:** 56, 58 Soi Piphat, North Sathorn Rd, Silom

Shewa Spa

Getting a foot massage at 7pm on the street while sipping a beer is the classic Thailand experience in this area. Even if you're not sippin a beer, the people watching is enough. Never underestimate how tired your feet will be after a long day of walking around Bangkok. This is the place to come!

☉ **Open:** 9am-1am
⟲ **How to Get There:** Walk through Susie Walking Street from Khao San to Rambuttri and you'll be spit out right at Shewa Spa on the left.
🚕 **Address:** 108, 1-3 Ram Buttri, Talat Yot, Phra Nakhon

Yunomori Onsen & Spa Bangkok

All of the baths! Detox your system by spending the day hopping from one hot bath to another in a calming, warmly lit atmosphere. Relax in the outdoor open-air garden bath, detoxify in the CO_2 soda bath, or get some "me time" in the individual teakwood bath. There is a spa on sight where many guests indulge in a 2-hour Thai massage or body scrubs to make their skin glow. If you don't know already, a traditional Japanese bath is communal- but separated by gender. I promise, it's not as awkward as it sounds.

☉ **Open:** 9am–Midnight, Book 48 hours in Advance!
💲 **Entrance Fee:** $13 USD/450 Baht (services not included)
⟲ **How to Get There:** BTS Phrom Phong, 1km away so take a taxi or Tuk Tuk
🚕 **Address:** A-Square 120/5 Soi Sukhumvit 26, Klongtoey

How to Move around Bangkok

BTS/MRT

From 5am–Midnight, hop on the most convenient form of air-conditioned travel that ever did exist. Everything is in English, easy to understand, clean, and safe. Taking the BTS or MRT is often much faster than taxing a taxi on the congested roads of Sukhumvit.

The MRT just opened up a new train line with 5 stops that connect Sukhumvit to the Khao San Road/Chinatown area of Bangkok.

NEED TO KNOW STOPS...

Remember, there are different train lines for both the BTS & MRT. Double check that you're getting on the correct direction. There are tons of easy-to-read maps in each station.

BTS

- **Asoke** – Terminal 21 Shopping Mall
- **Nana** – Red Light District
- **Chatuchak Market** – BTS Mo Chit (Exit 1)
- **National Stadium** – MBK Mall and GrabTaxi to Khao San Road
- **Siam** – The shopping district of Bangkok

MRT

- **Wat Mangkon** – Located close to Chinatown
- **Sanam Chai** – Temple of the Reclining Buddha and the Grand Palace in the Khao San Road Area
- **Itsaraphap** – Access the "Temple of Dawn" Wat Arun & Wang Lang Market

📍 **Thailand Cultural Center** – Ratchada Train Market

📍 **Chatuchak Weekend Market** – MRT Kamphaeng Phet, Exit 2

Taxis

Always use the meter in a taxi! The driver will try to give you a fixed rate (that's 3x the price) and will justify by saying things like "Oh so much traffic" or "Very far" but he's just trying to make an extra buck. Once the meter is on, you can trust that he'll take you where you need to go.

Grab Taxi

As I just mentioned, sometimes it can prove difficult to hail a taxi that doesn't want to rip you off, especially when you're in tourist areas. Skip the headache and order a Grab Taxi who will run the meter honestly, use GPS to find your location, and will drive much safer and slower than the taxi drivers who just don't give a shit. Sometimes the Grab Taxi is not a taxi, but a personal car like Uber. Grab Taxis are all around you so don't hesitate to take this safer option! There is even a Grab Van for airport transfers! Also download InDriver, it's like Grab Taxi but cheaper and you can "bid" how much you want to pay.

Tuk Tuks

Tuk Tuks are a fun experience but they are not for long distance journeys—more so for a day of sightseeing around Khao San Road or a 5 minute ride from the BTS to your hotel.

Unless you're taking this tour... ☞

Bus

These old school busses are the cheapest form of transport in Bangkok and a fun way to see the city! Your hotel can help you sort out which bus goes where. It's a leisurely ride so don't use them if you're in a hurry!

1-Day Itineraries for Bangkok

Mix and match these itineraries for a balanced Bangkok experience

THE ULTIMATE KHAO SAN ROAD EXPERIENCE

🕗 **8am** — Out of bed for breakfast at KC Guest House's Khao Man Gai stand or a fruit smoothie anywhere

🕘 **9am** — Head to Wat Pho with the Reclining Buddha - try to get a guide when you enter

🕙 **10am** — Walk to Tha Tien Express Boat Pier and take a river taxi across to Wat Arun and explore the temple

🕙 **10:45am** — Take a quick GrabTaxi to Wang Lang Market. Shop and snack your way through the market - but don't eat anything big!

🕧 **12:30pm** — Take a river taxi back towards the Grand Palace. Then take a tuk tuk (100 baht) to Khao San Road

🕐 **1pm** — Eat lunch at I Love Thai Food on Rambuttri Road

🕑 **2pm** — Collapse at your hotel

🕓 **4pm** — Reemerge for shopping on Khao San Road and Rambuttri Road
🕔 **5pm** — Get a beer and go sit in the foot massage chairs at Shewa Spa on Rambuttri - drink while people watching

🕔 **5:30pm** — Walk to the night market at the end of Rambuttri Road for dinner

🕕 **6:30pm** — Enjoy the antics on Khao San Road and then head to Ku Bar for a classy cocktail

LOCAL LIFE

⊙ **8am** — Join the Floating Market Tour with Pook or a Cooking Class with Poo & Friends

⊙ **1pm** — Go directly to Sabaijai Thai Massage

⊙ **2pm** — Head back to your hotel to rest and freshen up

⊙ **3pm** — Have linner (lunch/dinner) at I Love Thai Food

⊙ **5pm** — Go watch a Muay Thai Fight at any one of the 3 stadiums in town or head to the Flower Market

⊙ **7-8pm** — Taxi back to Ponta Tha Tien bar to have a beer or a late night bite while staring directly at Wat Arun glittering over the river (she's gorgeous at night) or go to Ku Bar

WEEKEND MARKET ADVENTURES

⊙ **9am to Noon** — Have a slow morning, get in the pool, get a massage, eat some street food.

⊙ **3pm** — Head to Chatuchak Market for shopping and eating.

⊙ **5pm** — Take a rest at Chatuchak Park where you can sit by the lake, eat some street snacks, and people watch

⊙ **6pm** — Take a GrabTaxi to Srinagarindra Train Night Market for more shopping, eating and drinking!

⊙ **9pm** — Got more energy? Head to Soi Cowboy and have a beer (go in one of the bars if you're brave enough)

bring a small backpack for carrying your shopping

SIGHTSEEING IN CHINATOWN

🕐 **10 am** — Have a light breakfast – no later than 10am.

🕐 **12pm** — Go for a morning massage to work out those sore feet

🕐 **3pm** — Chinatown Food Tour with Urban Adventures or walk to Wat Traimit (the golden temple)

🕐 **4pm** — Explore Chinatown on foot

🕐 **5pm** — Eat dinner at T&K Seafood

🕐 **6pm** — After the tour, visit Teens of Thailand Bar for to-die-for cocktails

CLASSIC SUKHUMVIT EXPERIENCE

🕐 **9am** — Take a cooking class with Poo or sign up in advance for a bike tour with 'Follow Me Bikes" to explore the outskirts of Bangkok

🕐 **3pm** — Back to the hotel to freshen up and relax

🕐 **5pm** — Head to Octave Rooftop Bar for Happy Hour

🕐 **6pm** — Go to dinner at Soi 38 Street Market or Tamnak Isan Restaurant

🕐 **7:30pm** — Walk around Nana District for people watching and shopping.

Still not sure what to do?

Have an itinerary that you want me to check?

Just want me to plan the whole damn thing for you?

♥ Visit TheSoloGirlsTravelGuide.com for trip planning options.

Chiang Mai

●————————————————●

BEST FOR:

Unplugging with floating bungalows, nature trekking and
jungle safaris

DAYS NEEDED:

3 nights minimum, 5 nights ideally

●————————————————●

CHIANG MAI

CHAPTER TWO
Chiang Mai

Elephants, jungles, and temple hikes- this gem of a city in the north of Thailand is loved and adored by all who visit.

Easy to navigate thanks to the ancient square fortress that surrounds the "Old City" and convenient to walk, Chiang Mai is a dream to just throw on a pair of shoes and explore. Inside and outside the fortress walls, you'll find accommodation for all budgets, lots of shopping nooks, and a little bit of partying, too.

Amenities here are a pleasant balance between the comforts of home and the exciting novelty of Thailand. You've got cafes with handcrafted coffee, bistros with western sandwiches made with local ingredients, and Thai food infused with northern flavors. There is ALWAYS a foodie adventure to be had.

It's easy to see why Chiang Mai is currently the 'digital nomad' center of the world. Prices are cheap, the city is safe, and meeting other travelers is a breeze. Many people come here for a quick vacay…and end up turning Chiang Mai into their second home.

Bring your sunscreen. Chiang Mai is a whirlwind of outdoor adventure.

AREAS TO EXPLORE IN CHIANG MAI

❶ Old City

The confines of Old City are surrounded by an ancient fortress wall and moat with ties to 13th century royal rivalries. All throughout the old city, you'll see historic temples, crumbling and worn away, standing right next to a brand new 7/11. You'll never tire of wandering Old City's streets amongst cafes, guest houses, restaurants, and the popular Sunday Night Market. This is the heart of Chiang Mai.

❷ Nimman

Outside the Northeast Corner of the Old City is Nimman—the Digital Nomad Zone. Here is where waves of international expats have come to settle down for a few months or a few years. You'll find tons of western food, lots of vegan options, and the giant shopping mall called Maya Mall that satisfies the western and vegetarian palate.

③ Loi Kroh Road + Night Bazaar

Home to the daily Night Bazaar, Loi Kroh Road comes alive as soon as the sun starts to set. This street is lined with stalls selling souvenirs, street food vendors, and bars with bar girls playing pool with old white dudes. It's an entertaining place to have a wander.

📷 @DUCKMAN1992

Getting into Chiang Mai

✈ FROM CHIANG MAI AIRPORT

Finally, an airport that is actually in the city! Only 10–15 minutes from the center.

○ *Option 1:* Take a Grab Taxi

With so many guesthouses in Chiang Mai, the most hassle-free way to get from the airport is to just program your route into GPS and let a car pick you up at the curb.

🎟 *How much:* 50–160 Baht depending on your hotel

○ *Option 2:* **Airport Taxi**

If you don't have data on your phone, take a standard taxi.

♀ **Where:** There are two taxi Kiosks in the airport terminal where you can organize your ride, or simply walk outside the airport to the left, and wait for someone to yell "taxi!"

🎫 **How much:** 160 Baht flat charge per car

PRO TIP! Confirm the price with the taxi driver, "160 Baht, Na?"—just so they know that you know the correct price.

○ *Option 3:* **Take a Songthaew**

In Chiang Mai, Songthaews are trucks where you sit on little benches in the back. You tell the driver your destination, and he takes you to your location, as he drops others riders off one-by-one. The driver will tell you when it's your stop OR you can press the little buzzer if you see your stop.

♀ **Where:** Walk to the outside gates of the airport, where you'll see a little covered bus stop with Thai people waiting. A Songthaew will pull up here every 20 minutes or so.

🎫 **How Much:** 40–60 Baht per person

🕐 **Time:** Songthaews stop operating just before midnight

✈ FROM CHIANG MAI TRAIN STATION

The train station is located about 3km outside the city center—super convenient.

○ *Option 1:* **Public Transport**

When you walk outside, you'll be bombarded by a line of Thai men offering tuk tuks, taxis, and Songthaews. You've just got to pick your price point.

🎫 **Songthaew:** 40 Baht (although, they might push you to 60 Baht)

🎫 **Tuk Tuk:** 150 Baht

🎫 **Taxi:** 200 Baht

○ *Option 2:* **Grab Taxi**

Important: The public transport drivers don't like Grab Taxi encroaching on their territory at the Train Station. Simply, cross the street and go to a local café before you call your Grab to avoid conflict. Be discrete.

💵 **How Much:** 80–200 Baht depending on your hotel's location

✈ FROM ARCADE BUS STATION

○ *Option 1:* **Songthaews**

Confirm your location and price with the driver before you get in!

📍 **Where:** You'll find Songthaews near Terminal 3
💵 **How Much:** 20–60 Baht

○ *Option 2:* **Tuk Tuk**

Plenty of Tuk Tuks will be competing for your attention once you get off the bus! Now's your chance to haggle.

💵 **How Much:** 80–100 Baht

FUN THAI FACT!
It was two Thai brothers that inspired the term "Siamese Twins" as they were conjoined at the chest when the country was named "Siam" in the 1800's.

BONUS ADVENTURE...

Before Coming to Chiang Mai

If you have a day or two to spare, consider stopping in the ancient town of Ayutthaya before you head up to Chiang Mai from Bangkok.

The second Siamese Capitol after Sukhothai, Ayutthaya was built in 1350 with grandiose temples, towers, and relics...until the Burmese destroyed the city. Today, Ayutthaya's remains are well preserved, offering a glimpse into a civilization that once was.

Take the train to Ayutthaya from Bangkok on your way to Chiang Mai. Stay in the guest house called Baan Thai House. Go on an evening boat cruise along the river. In the morning, hop in a tuk tuk for an ancient tour you've got to see to believe.

Don't want to do it DIY?
Here's a fabulous tour that does the planning for you!

📷 @POPAREM

Where to Stay in Chiang Mai

Hey! Keep in mind that other girls with this book will be staying at the same hotels and hostels as you! Keep an eye out for a solo travel sister!

PRO TIP! If you're up for traveling an hour away from the city to sleep in a glass-ceiling glamping tent on the river, check out Morning Star Glamping. If you're up for tree houses that are 1.5 hours away, look into Tree House Hideaway Chiang Mai.

Four Seasons Chiang Mai

If you want to get off the beaten path without driving hours into the jungle, this is the perfect compromise. One of the most beautiful hotels in Chiang Mai, Four Seasons Chiang Mai sits on a pure piece of land surrounded by lush green trees and tropical flowers that lull you into relaxation. Enjoy gorgeous pools that look out onto rice fields, kind of reminiscent of Bali. Take in the pure nature that surrounds you. Indulge in the on-site spa. Go for a walk in the fields. This is paradise.

★*Style:* Privates
Budget: $$$$
Where: Mae Rim

BOOK HERE

Baan Boo Loo Village

You must stay here for at least one night! Baan Boo Loo Village is one of the most unique hotel concepts I have ever come across! The hotel is made up of old wooden houses that have been pieced together in a fairytale-come-to-life manner, and decorated like a Thai art gallery and museum. The hotel is owned, operated and built by a Thai family who put love into everything they do, including taking care of you. This place is a bucket-list must!

★*Style:* Privates
💸*Budget:* $$$
📍*Where:* Old City

BOOK HERE

Lamphu House Chiang Mai

When you want privacy and a pool, but are on a budget, this is where you come. My vote for the best solo girl hotel in Chiang Mai is Lamphu House. Dreamy beds, a fabulous pool, and amazing location within walking distance to Tha Phae Gate, right next to the big Sunday Night Market, and surrounded by some of the best restaurants in the city. After you're done exploring, go collapse on a lounge chair by the pool. And in full transparency...if you're planning to go on Tinder, this place has enough privacy for you to bring a boy back to your room. Speaking from experience...

★*Style:* Privates
💸*Budget:* $$
📍*Where:* Old City

BOOK HERE

Pastell Oldtown Chiang Mai

A super clean, charming and comfy hotel perfect for a solo girl. This brand-new hotel has all of the modern amenities including a pool! Step outside and you'll be surrounded by restaurants, massage parlors, and night markets. What I love most about this place is the staff who will help you arrange anything you need.

★*Style:* Privates
💸*Budget:* $$
📍*Where:* Southwest Old Town

BOOK HERE

BED Nimman – Adults Only

No kids allowed! You don't have to worry about this pool getting overrun with splashing children. BED Nimman is a modern hotel with chic décor, cloud-comfy beds, excellent service, free water, and a healthy buffet breakfast. Take note, BED Nimman is located in the more modern Digital Nomad Zone. So if you're looking to move to Chiang Mai or are working while you travel, this is a great place to use a homebase to get to know the expat scene here.

★ **Style:** Privates
Budget: $$
Where: Nimman

BOOK HERE

Suneta Hostel Chiang Mai

You will drink at this hostel but still keep your dignity. There are tons of hostels in Chiang Mai that are just downright sleazy...but this is not one of them. Yes, you will make friends who want to go out and party with you but you will not be kept up until 3am by the sounds of drinking contests downstairs.

★ **Style:** Dorms and Very Small Private Rooms
Budget: $
Where: Central as can be!
Right outside the Old City Gate

BOOK HERE

The Entaneer Poshtel

A posh hostel = Poshtel! After a long day of elephant tours and temple hikes, all you want to do is chill out in a laid back hostel with some laid back people. The Entaneer Poshtel is famous for being a low-key social spot where you can easily meet other travelers without excessive drinking. The wifi is fast, the hostel is gorgeous, and the location is within walking distance to WuaLai Walking Street and the Saturday Market.

★ **Style:** Dorms and Privates
Budget: $
Where: Just South of the Old City gates

BOOK HERE

Shopping in Chiang Mai

Saturday Walking Market

Scarves, paintings, lanterns, and silver jewelry line the streets of the Saturday Market—but, you'll have to elbow your way through the crowd of people to have a look. The market is laid out on one very narrow street where you can expect to be shoulder to shoulder with other tourists. The saving grace is the outdoor food court with sit-down tables. If you don't mind crowds—go for it. If not, wait til Sunday…

⊙ **Open:** 5pm–10pm. Get there around 4:30 to beat the crowds.
♥ **Where:** Wualai Rd just outside the Old City
↻ **How to Get There:** Walk or take a Grab Taxi to the Southern Gate Wall. You'll see the crowds!

Sunday Market

Right in the center of Old City is the Sunday Walking Street. With two wide lanes, you can take your time strolling around while you visit stalls with handmade jewelry, artisan soaps, and little souvenirs. The street is lined with a couple of Buddhist Temples that open up into day-time food markets with every Thai food under the sun. When your feet are tired, there are rows and rows of comfy chairs for 150 Baht foot massages. Go crazy.

⊙ **Open:** 5pm–10pm. Get there around 4:30 to beat the crowds.
♥ **Where:** Ratchadamnoen Rd stretches from Tha Phae Gate and Wat Phra Singh temple.
↻ **How to Get There:** The road is huge and you can intersect it at many junctions. It's easiest to start at Tha Phae Gate.

Warorot Market

A true Thai Flea Market, Warorot Market is a 3 story facility divided into sections selling teapots, dried fruit, skin care, fabrics, live amphibious creatures, and so much more. The few blocks that surround Warorot are lined with stalls selling random things like flashlights and fishing nets across the street from big beauty stores and cheap clothing stores. Go have a wander and sample some food along the way.

☉ **Open:** 4am–6pm
🚉 **Address:** 90 Wichayanon Rd.
☾ **How to Get There:** Hop in a red Songthaew for 40 Baht

MALLS

There are 7 malls in Chiang Mai; each one a little different from the next. Here are the top 3…

Maya Mall

Located in the Nimman Area, Maya has an amazing food court in the basement, popular stores like NYX Makeup & American Eagle, has a modern movie theater with the latest releases and an open-air rooftop with bars and live music.

Central Festival

About a 20 minute Grab Taxi from the Old City, Central Festival is where you go to restock on the basics from home. There is an H&M, Zara, Uniqlo and a few trendier stores. The basement has a collection of Thai teas, dried fruit, and small-business shops.

Central Kad Suan Kaew

This old-school Thai mall is more of a cultural experience than a shopping-spree destination. Conveniently located in the Nimman area, it's worth a look if you want to grab an ice cream at Dairy Queen or a Starbucks coffee. There are tons of low-priced Thai clothing stores but the sizes are targeted towards slim Thai girls with no boobies.

PLEASE DON'T DO THIS!!!!

At the start of the 20th century Thailand had over 100,000 Asian elephants; today it's estimated that there are just around 4,000 elephants left, of which only 1,500 live in the wild.

Want to help those numbers increase? Say no to elephant riding establishments. Support elephant sanctuaries.

FUN FACT! Elephants in captivity individually choose their human friend. These friends/caretakers are called Mahouts.

✐ JOURNAL PROMPT

My favorite people I've met on this trip:

Things To Do in Chiang Mai

Elephant Sanctuaries

The original Elephant Sanctuary in Chiang Mai is called 'Elephant Nature Park', run & founded by a Thai woman named Lek. This little lady crusader has rescued injured, old, and abandoned elephants from street begging, overworked logging jobs, and tourist-fed elephant riding establishments.

Visiting the park truly is a once in a lifetime experience. You get to interact with the elephants, taking long walks, hand feeding them fruit, and even bathing with them in the river—without disrupting their schedule or exploiting their existence. To visit, book your tour weeks in advance. In the event that this sanctuary is all booked up, then check out Elephant Jungle Sanctuary or Bees Elephant Sanctuary (very rural with Thai-style accommodation).

@MEAGANSTANS

💰 **Entrance Fee:** Budget $77 USD/2,500 Baht
🕐 **Open:** Everyday, time depends on your tour
📍 **Where:** Mountains in Chiang Mai
↻ **How to Get There:** Free pickup from your hotel in Chiang Mai

---

♥ **Elephant Sanctuary Rule of Thumb:** If an elephant park offers elephant rides, they are not a sanctuary.

Sticky Waterfalls

Take a nature stroll through bright green bamboo trails until you reach Sticky Waterfalls (Bua Thong Waterfalls). Grab onto a rope start climbing up the 500 meter cascading falls! It's not too intense, don't worry.

💰 **Entrance Fee:** Donation Box
📍 **Where:** 60km in the Mountains of Chiang Mai
↻ **How to Get There:** 1.5 hour ride via motorbike or hire a Songthaew/Taxi and haggle a price depending on how many people are in your group (maybe 120 Baht/person round trip).

PS. Food & drink is not allowed inside. Just water bottles.

Doi Kham Temple

Also known as Wat Phra That Doi Kham, this temple is totally worth the 30 minute adventure south of the city center. Standing at 17 meters high with a uniquely draped golden shall, this is easily one of the most impressive Buddhist Temples in Thailand. Off the beaten path, you can expect a more local crowd who comes to pray for good student grades and lucky lotto tickets. As with many temples, you'll find stalls with local Thai snacks and souvenirs outside the temple on the top of the hill.

💰 **Entrance Fee:** Free

↻ **How to Get There:**

> If you're an experienced motorbike driver, slap on a helmet and drive up the steep winding mountain.

> Order a Grab Taxi who will drive you to the top of the mountain. You can take a Songthaew back down the mountain into town.

> Hike from the base of the mountain up a 20–30 minute natural staircase. You can find the entrance where the Songthaews hang out.

PRO TIP! At the base of the mountain, you'll see stalls selling strings of flowers to give as an offering to Buddha (and supporting small entrepreneurs)—starting at 1 Baht.

Doi Suthep Temple

You can see the glittering temple of Doi Suthep 1,600 meters below in the city center. Once you get to the base of Doi Suthep, you'll find a road buzzing with small shops selling scarves, trinkets, and waffle hotdogs (yum). Climb up the 300 or so steps to the temple, with little Hmong Children lining the stairs trading photos for cash. Expect towering golden temples, the scent of incense burning, and the little pockets of Buddhist statues where locals go to pray. Once you've had your spiritual moment, visit the breathtaking viewpoint where you can see the entirety of the city while watching planes taking off the airport.

💰 *Entrance Fee:* $1 USD/30 Baht
↻ *How to Get There:*

> Experienced motorbike drivers can enjoy the windy drive up the mountain, stopping at a café at the base of the mountain afterwards

> Order a Grab Taxi

> Take a 50 Baht Songthaew from the Northern Gate Market, corner of Manee Nopparat Rd & Changhuak Rd

> Set off on a gorgeous, yet challenging 2–3 hour hike starting at the base

Wat Rong Khun – The White Temple

Right out of a Disney movie, this whimsical 20th century Buddhist Temple is a one-of-a-kind artistic tribute to Buddhism, the afterlife, and eastern mythology everywhere you look. To get there, you'll have to take a full-day trip to Chiang Rai, a town about 3 hours north of Chiang Mai. Tours include a private driver and usually, some extra trips to Doi Kham or a boat ride on a local river. Ask your hostel or hotel to help you book!

💸 **Entrance Fee:** 50 Baht
💸 **Full-Day Tour Prices:** Starts at $55 USD/1,800 Baht

Gibbon Experience

Become one with your inner monkey as your climb through the trees on wooden bridges, zipline through the canopy, and repel down to the floor. The 2½ hour tour includes the canopy tour, lunch and a waterfall walk. It's an exhilarating experience led by professionals who no stranger to the occasional 'fear of heights' freak out.

💸 **Budget:** $130 USD/4,199 Baht
⊙ **Tour Times:** 6:30am, 8am, 9am, 12:30pm
♥ **Where:** Mountains in Chiang Mai
⟳ **How to Get There:** Free pickup from your hotel.

Get a Massage from Female Prisoners

Yes, you read that right. As part of their rehabilitation, female prisoners are being trained in massage at the Vocational Training Center Of Chiang Mai Women's Correctional Institution. The prices are super fair starting at 200 baht an hour - but I recommend treating yourself with a 2-hour massage that will really drain the toxins out of your body.

⊙ **Open:** 8am-4pm
♥ **Where:** Inside old town
🏛 **Address:** Jhaban Rd x Ratviti Rd
📞 **Call ahead:** +66 53 122 340

Chiang Mai Cabaret Show

You've never seen anyone more glamorous than a Thai Ladyboy—and damn, do they know how to put on a show. Iconic musical impersonations with wardrobes that are to die for and choreography straight off Broadway, this Cabaret show is incredible. Your entrance fee comes with one free drink, too. What a bargain.

⊙ **Open:** Daily 9:30pm
💵 **Entrance Fee:** $11 USD/350 Baht
📍 **Where:** Anusarn Market, Night Bazaar
↻ **How to Get There:** Head towards the night bazaar & Loi Kroh Stadium

The Thai and Akha Cooking School

Thai Style Cooking with a sprinkle of Akha Hill Tribe Flair, this cooking class offers a unique local experience off the tourist path. During your cooking class, you'll prepare 11 different dishes, including a combination of soups, desserts, appetizers and entrees in a outdoor Thai kitchen! You'll learn each step of the process, including shopping for ingredients at the local market (morning class).

💵 **Budget:** $30 USD/1,000 Baht
⊙ **Class Times:** Everyday 8:30 & 4:30
📍 **Where:** Northeast Corner of the Old City
↻ **How to Get There:** Free pick-up and drop-off from your hotel!

Grand Canyon Water Park

There is a massive manmade gorge just 20 minutes south of the center which has been turned into an Thai-style waterpark with a floating obstacle course, water slide, and massive blob that catapults you into the air. There is a restaurant on site, lockers, and lounge chairs to catch some fun.

💵 **Entrance Fee:** $10 USD/300 Baht
⊙ **Open:** Everyday 10am–7pm
📍 **Where:** Grand Canyon Chiang Mai
↻ **How to Get There:** Take a tuk tuk for about 600 Baht each way.

Top 5 Tours in Chiang Mai

Even for people who don't usually like tours…

01 Elephant Sanctuary with Rescued Elephants from around Thailand

For a smaller, more intimate experience, visit **Lanna Elephant**

 For more elephants and volunteering, visit **Elephant Nature Park**

02 Sticky Waterfalls and **Doi Suthep Temple**

 03 Take a (Long) Day Trip to the **White Temple** in Chiang Rai

04 Take a Private Tuk Tuk Tour of **Chiang Mai's Temples with a Guide**

 05 Explore **Rural Chiang Mai** in a Tuk Tuk

Where To Eat In Chiang Mai

Chiang Mai is a street food city! But there are a couple really great restaurants scattered around the city, so here we go...

 **BREAKFAST & LUNCH**

Blue Diamond Breakfast Club

Wake up slowly as you sit in a tranquil botanical garden with a waterfall feature and cool breeze. Sip on freshly squeezed juice and snack on vegan muffins or vegetarian omelets. Before you go, check out the Blue Diamond storefront where you can take home organic jam or homemade donuts for a yummy afternoon snack.

🕐 *Open:* 7:30am–8pm
🚉 *Address:* 35/1 MoonMuang Rd, Soi 9

Ginger & Kafe

This upscale Thai bistro with vegan & vegetarian options offers a rustic yet elegant oasis in the middle of Chiang Mai. Here's your chance to try elevated Thai dishes with a twist on the classics. Try hand-tied dumplings with sweet plum sauce, colorful fresh spring rolls with Thai mango and shrimp, or chicken satay skewers with peanut sauce. The dishes here is plated so beautifully that they are sure to wind up all over your Instagram.

🕐 *Open:* Fri–Thu 10am–11pm
🚉 *Address:* 199, Moonmuang Rd, Tambon Si Phum

Maya Mall Basement Food Court

Food courts in Thailand offer the best street food style dishes prepared in the cleanest kitchens for the best price and Maya Mall's food court is no exception. They've got all the best Thai dishes—vegetarian stalls included—but the real star of this place is Wrap Master…the best burritos in town starting at 80 Baht.

🕐 **Open:** Daily 11am–9pm
🚇 **Address:** 55 Huay Kaew Rd

 DINNER

Lert Ros

You guys! You cannot come to Chiang Mai and not eat at Lert Ros. Lert—the man himself—is manning the grills every night with massive grilled fish, shrimp, beef, and pork that come with amazing sauces—it's all about the sauces! Order a hot bowl of Tom Yum Soup and a side of Som Tom Salad and you're set for life. Plus the food is cheap! Walk away spending around 360 Baht for 2 people (with beers, duh).

🕐 **Open:** Sun–Sat (closed Mon) 12pm–9pm
🚇 **Address:** Soi 1, Ratchadamneon Rd

📷 **LERT ROS**

The Salsa Kitchen

Crunchy corn tortilla tacos, legit enchiladas, and some damn fine margaritas, The Salsa Kitchen hits the spot when you're in the mood for Mexican. The ambiance is a relaxed sit-down space with attentive service. And the best part, food portions are huge so you can expect to take some food to go.

⊙ **Open:** Daily 11am–11pm
🏠 **Address:** 26/4 Huay Kaew Rd

Tong Tem Toh

Issan is the largest region in Thailand and also the poorest. As Isaan workers migrated to the big cities for work, Isaan restaurants started to pop up everywhere! You can experience Northern dishes at this family-owned and operated Isaan restaurant in Nimman where steamed fish, grilled pork, and traditional fried morning glory are the stars. 10 extra points for ambiance and service!

⊙ **Open:** Sun 11am–11pm, Mon 9am–9pm, Tue–Thu 11am–9pm & Fri–Sat 11am–11pm
🏠 **Address:** Nimmana Haeminda 13

Mad Dog Pizza

The cheesiest, most self-indulgent pizza you will find in Thailand, Mad Dog is where it's at. They are so generous with sauce and toppings! Even the small size pizza is pretty damn big. They've got beer on tap and sports on the flat screens—pull up a stool at the bar and dig in. And if you're really hungry…the chicken wings are killer.

⊙ **Open:** 8am–11pm
🏠 **Address:** 9/3 Mun Mueang Rd

NIGHTMARKETS

Chiang Mai Gate Night Market

From the grill to the wok- everything Thai can be found at this quaint night market sitting over the moat with about 30 stalls total. With plenty of tables and chairs, you can collect dishes from several stands and create a feast! Stock up on beers at the 7/11 across the street!

⊙ **Open:** Daily 6pm - 11pm
🛒 **Address:** 87 Bumrung Buri Rd

Chiang Mai Night Bazaar

Snack on crispy spring rolls or coconut ice cream as you wander the streets of Chiang Mai Night Bazaar. Head into the food court for the full spread of Chinese-inspired noodles, Mango Sticky Rice and every Thai curry you could ever imagine. When you're done, walk it off as you browse through an endless line of souvenir stalls with soft scarves and tiny carved elephants.

⊙ **Open:** Daily 6pm - 11pm
🛒 **Address:** Between Loi Kroh Rd and Tha Phae Rd
↻ **How to Get There:** Walk down one of those roads and you'll intersect the market.

North Gate Night Market

Once the sun starts to set, this little night market comes alive. From the best Khoa Kha Moo in the city to authentic middle eastern Roti- there's tons to eat here. You'll also find lots of fresh fruit and vegetarian options! Afterwards, head towards the massage shop at the back of the market and embrace your food coma.

⊙ **Open:** Daily 6pm - 11pm
🛒 **Address:** Manee Nopparat Rd.
↻ **How to Get There:** Head towards the north gate- the market is right over the moat next to Buaraya Hotel.

Saturday Walking Street (Wualai Walking Street)

One narrow road that gets crowded as hell! If you don't mind the crowds, this night market has a lot to offer. There's artwork, souvenirs and of course, food! Plus, it's very conveniently located so you won't be taking a huge chunk of time off from your night if you decide to stop by.

🕗 **Open:** Saturday 6:30pm - 10:30pm
🚇 **Address:** Wua Lai Road
🚶 **How to Get There:** Head South of Old City, cross through the Chiang Mai Gate Market and you'll find Wulai Road on the other side!

Nightlife in Chiang Mai

Like every tourist town, you can find lots of laid-back bars with beer, nachos, and pool tables by just having a wander. But if you want to get a bit wild and mingle with other travelers, follow the Chiang Mai nightlife loop where the crowd migrates together from one spot to the next.

Zoe in Yellow

The party starts here. At around 9 o'clock, the collection of bars that make up the Zoe in Yellow court start to fill up. There is a big courtyard with picnic tables, some smaller establishments where you can pull up a stool at the bar, and a couple bars with a dance floor. By midnight, the partiers spill into the middle of Zoe for a mingling session before they migrate to the next location together.

🕗 **Open:** Daily 9pm–Midnight
🚇 **Address:** Rajvithi Rd

Spicy

Next up, the crowd moves to Spicy—the warehouse nightclub with a live DJ, lazer lights, and a dance floor. Beers are a bit overpriced and the place gets super packed—but if you're looking for a bit of flirty fun, here is where you'll find it.

🕐 **Open:** Opens at 9 but the real party doesn't start til after midnight.
🚉 **Address:** Chayaphum Rd

Living Room

End the night at Living Room. With a bit of a dingy college party feel, this 'underground' after hours club has two pool tables, a smoking area, and a college-esque bar pumping mingle music. The catch? This place closes it's metal gate outside to appear closed as bars are not allowed to be open past 2am. Ps. Your admissions ticket counts for 1 drink.

🕐 **Open:** 9pm–5am
🚉 **Address:** 5, 95 Sithiwongse Rd

Club Mandalay

Imagine the hit TV show 'The Voice' with the big stage, the professional lights, and the passion that pours out of the singers! Mandalay's show is full of energy with Thai singers covering English songs from Rock Classics to Modern Gaga. Get a table, order a bottle, and know that the 200 Baht cover is totally worth it. Bring your ID to get in.

🕐 **Open:** 10pm–2am
🚉 **Address:** 5/3 Moon Muang Rd Lane 2

Spas in Chiang Mai

City Nails

City Nails does it all—simple gel nails, glittery deco nails, pedicures, eyelash extensions, eyelash tinting and waxing. They are super professional, very hygienic, and great at what they do. Plus, their prices aren't bad either.

🕐 *Open:* Daily 10am–8pm
🏛 *Address:* 49/1–8 Arak Rd. T.Phra Singh

Robin Beauty Bar

The best (and cheapest) waxing service in town—Robin Beauty Bar is popular with western expats, and tourists alike. Kung is the expert waxer who uses a mixture of homemade wax and humor to make the experience less painful and more entertaining. You'll pay 1/3 of what you would at home with 100 Baht eye brow waxes and 600 Baht Brazilians! It's best to call ahead to make an appointment but you might get lucky with a walk in—the salon near Tha Phae Gate.

🕐 *Open:* Mon–Sat 10am–6:30pm & Sun 12pm–6:30pm
🏛 *Address:* Moon Muang Rd Lane 8

New York New York

When you need a root touch up, a good wash, some deep conditioning, or want a total color makeover—this is the place to trust. An Aveda Salon with experienced professionals who have been doing western hair for decades and are constantly studying their craft—it's just like being in the chair at home.

🕐 *Open:* Daily 10am–10pm
🏛 *Address:* Nimman Haeminda Rd Lane 13, Tambon Su Thep

Moving Around Chiang Mai

Chiang Mai is relatively small and in theory, you can walk from one corner of the city to the next. But girl, it can get sweaty.

Songthaew

When you see one of these red trucks driving down the road, just wave your arm, run up to their driver-side window to tell them your destination and hop in the back. The standard rate is 20 Baht per person, but if you're going from one end of the city to the next, expect a haggle up to 60 Baht.

Grab Taxi

Sign up for Grab Taxi and you'll get tons of promotion texts with promo codes. You can literally get rides for free (I did for almost an entire month).

Tuk Tuk

Tuk Tuks are everywhere. It's up to you to haggle your price. You won't usually get lower than 80 Baht per ride.

FUN THAI FACT!
Chiang Mai is Thailand's second largest city, after Bangkok.

Where Next After Chiang Mai?

You're in the north, close to so many cool locations - if you have the time to see them. If you had just one week left - I'd say go to Khao Sok or Railay. But if your trip is open ended, pencil these two places in...

Sukhothai

On your way back down south to Bangkok, make a pit stop in the ancient city of Sukhothai.

Built during a revolt against the Khmer Rule somewhere between the years 1238 and 1257, this UNESCO World Heritage Site eventually served as the Thai capital during the 13th Century C.E.

The entire site covers approximately 27 square miles and is divided into multiple zones featuring fortress moats, bridges and walls, lakes that reflect ancient architecture like a mirror, ancient Buddhist statues, and royal buildings with mysterious winding staircases and small temples around every corner.

Although Sukhothai was built one century later, you can certainly see the Khmer inspired-architecture reminiscent of Cambodia's Angkor Wat—yet, on a smaller, less crowded scale.

↻How to Get There: You can take a 4.5–5 hour bus from Chiang Mai's Arcade Bus Station. There are 10 buses that leave every day between 7am and 5:30pm. Or you can take a train from Chiang Mai to Sawankhalok Station, 30 km from Sukhothai where Songthaews will be waiting to transport you.

Pai & Mae Hong Son Loop

Most tourists don't know about this unspoiled, jungley part of Thailand—which makes it one of the best kept secrets. The Pai & Mae Hong Son Loop is a 4 day, 600km long motorbike circuit that takes you to both cities via an absolutely breathtaking road.

First described to me as "a beach town in the jungle", Pai is this laidback hippie town with sprawling mountain roads perfect for renting a motorbike to explore the nearby waterfalls or rice paddies. At night, stroll the night market, eat some burgers, or chill out with live music.

Next, visit Mae Hong Son—the tiny Burmese border town where you can sample Burmese food and culture. Hike up to Wat Phrathat Doi Kongmu for a gorgeous sunrise over the entire city.

Here's a mini Pai Bucket List:
- ◯ Stay at JJ Garden
- ◯ Walking Street every Night
- ◯ Sianam Hot Springs
- ◯ Pai Canyon for Sunset
- ◯ Bamboo Bridge
- ◯ Eat and Drink at…
- ◯ Coffee at Art in Chai
- ◯ Eat at Thai-Zen Organic Farm
- ◯ Cocktails at Spirit bar

↻*How to Get There:* Only drive the loop if you are comfortable on a motorbike. The roads can get pretty windy and it's a 4-day drive...so you have to be really stoked to do it. If you're not comfortable on a bike, you can easily visit Pai and Mae Hong Son via minivan. Just visit a tour company to hook you up.

HOW TO GET TO OTHER DESTINATIONS FROM CHIANG MAI...

Chiang Mai has mountains, elephants, and laid back vibes and serves as digital nomad central! You can also use Chiang Mai as a jumping off point to Pai or Mae Hong Son.

○ *Option 1:* **By Sleeper Train**

A must-have experience if you've got time! The Sleeper Train is comfortable, affordable, and saves you one night's accommodation. Buy your tickets at least 2 days in advance! You can do this via a travel agency or by going directly to the station.

Go with the 2nd class fan option. 1st class is just the same but blasts the air conditioning so high that it's a miserably cold ride.

Try to get a bottom bunk! They are more comfortable and you don't have to climb a ladder to go to the bathroom in the middle of the night!

If you're visiting during Thai holidays, buy your train tickets as early as you can. You can book 1 month in advance!

♥ *Point of Departure:* Hua Lamphong Station
⊙ *When:* 8:30am, 1:45pm, 6:10pm, 7:30pm, 10pm
⊙ *Duration:* 13–14 hours
💵 *Budget:* $18 USD/590 Baht

○ *Option2:* **By Plane**

⚲ Point of Departure: BKK/SVB or DMK

☉ Duration: 1 hour & 10 minutes

⚑ Budget: $60 USD/2,000 Baht

○ *Option 3:* **By Bus**

⚲ Point of Departure: Mo Chit Bus Terminal (Northern Bus Terminal)

☉ When: Every hour between 5:30am and 10pm

☉ Duration: Roughly 10 hours

⚑ Budget: $16 USD/530 Baht

TRAVEL NOTES:

....

....

....

....

....

....

....

CHAPTER THREE

Khao Sok

BEST FOR:

Unplugging with floating bungalows, nature trekking and jungle safaris

DAYS NEEDED:

3 nights minimum, 5 nights ideally

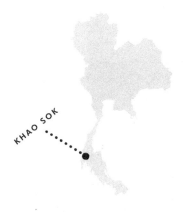

CHAPTER THREE

Khao Sok

I beg of you, please add Khao Sok to your Thailand itinerary. If you don't, you will be missing out on one of the most unique, majestic experiences a human being can have on Earth.

I know none of your friends have heard of this place and not even many Thai people know about Khao Sok because that is just how unspoiled and untouched this region is!

Khao Sok is Thailand's own Halong Bay, hidden between limestone cliffs jetting out from a glowing blue lake. The lake is surrounded by the world's oldest evergreen forest which is estimated to be 160 million years old - that's older than the Amazon rainforest. Khao Sok and its national park is one of the best preserved forested regions in the entire world, teeming with diverse species of monkeys, flora, fauna, and 311 different kinds of birds.

Coming here feels like visiting another realm of reality, one in which the earth was never developed or discovered. It's complete peace. It's heaven on Earth. Best of all, you can sleep on floating bungalows in the middle of the lake under the stars away from the outside world - only accessible by a one-hour boat ride.

Here, you are free.

Before you head to the lake, you will first arrive in Khao Sok town, a quaint village where time slows down. There's a river that runs through town, lined with gorgeous treehouse hotels. And there's a small road that runs through town, lined with little guesthouses, restaurants and a couple garden bars. You'll spend a day or two playing on the river and exploring the forest - with drinks and pizza at night. And you'll spend one day exploring the lake by longtail boat and kayak. It feels like summer camp.

It's really simple to plan a trip here. Your hotel books all your adventures - including your over-water bungalows since they're owned by the National Park.

And so, this is going to be a short chapter because it's an easy destination. You just show up and the rest falls into place.

Things To Do in Khao Sok

Sleep in Bungalows on the Lake

Sleep in the super-simple floating bungalows owned by Khao Sok National Park. I met 12 other travelers on this overnight excursion which felt like an adult summer camp. Unlike me who was beginning my trip in Khao Sok, most of them were ending their trip in Khao Sok. After traveling to islands and the cities all around Thailand, the consensus was that this overnight experience was the highlight of almost everyone's trip.

PRO TIP! Bring your own beers, a mini speaker, sunscreen, tevas or water shoes for the hike, a dry bag, a quick dry towel, and some extra snacks if you wish.

Go on a Night Safari

A truck will pick you up once night falls. You'll climb in the back and be taken to the national park with your guide. Together, you will walk through the jungle along the main path - or off the beaten path if you so choose - following the guide's flashlight as he points out owls eating frogs, hairy caterpillars as big as a hot dog, jungle cats - if you're lucky, and many more wild creatures of the night.

Bamboo River Rafting

Float down on a bamboo raft with a captain propelling you along with a stick. You'll weave underline stone cliffs and gasp at their beauty. You'll stop at a little hut on the side of the river where your guide will make you coffee over a fire, the jungle way. You'll stop at a tree that you can rope swing off of into the water.

River Floating in Inner Tubes

When the river water is high enough, you can float down with your but in the water and a cold beer in your hand.

Explore the Town

Khao Sok has one main road that stretches from the national park outwards into civilization, although you'll only be walking a short stretch of it (no civilization for you). You'll find reggae bars with pool tables and smokable things, massage parlors, pizza places, live music and everything else you need to slow down and enjoy the travel life.

And that's it! Sure, your guesthouses might offer a cooking class or bird watching experience - but these are the true bucket list items to tick in Khao Sok. Simple, peaceful and oh-so charming.

Where to Stay in Khao Sok

You're going on the overnight lake trip right? Right? You better be!

Almost all guesthouses and hostels sell the overnight package like this:

2 nights / 3 days which includes 1 night at their accommodation and 1 night on the lake.

You can book that now, if you want…but that bundle feels rushed to me. Instead, here's how I recommend you book your Khao Sok Trip:

○ **Step 1:** Book a hotel for your first 2 nights in Khao Sok. Wait til you arrive in Khao Sok to book your overnight stay at the bungalows.

○ **Step 2:** When you arrive, tell your hotel that you'd like to do a sleepover on the bungalows. You will arrange this tour plus your other tours at the hotel.

○ **Step 3:** Book a different hotel after your bungalows. A new hotel gives you a totally new Khoa Sok experience.

So your trip looks like this:

✳ First 2 nights at Hotel #1

✳ 1 night on the overwater bungalows

✳ Next 2 nights at Hotel #2

…or if you're in a rush, ignore everything I've just said and go with the 2 nights/3 days package. Anyways - I'll give you my ultimate Khao Sok itinerary to follow step-by-step at the end of this chapter.

First - let's pick where you're going to stay for your first 2 nights.

Our Jungle House

Treehouse alert! I want to live here forever. Our Jungle House is the perfect balance of off-the-grid and plugged in. On one hand, you sleep in tree houses and walk amongst nature and fireflies. On the other, you're just a short walk to town. I've traveled all over Thailand and have even lived here for years, and this was one of the most magical Thailand experiences I've ever had. I can't recommend them enough.

★ **Style:** Treehouses over the river
💰 **Budget:** $$
📍 **Where:** Tucked off the main street - 7 minute walk

BOOK HERE

Our Jungle Camp

Our Jungle Camp is the sister location to Our Jungle House, just a stone's throw away. When I visited Khao Sok, I stayed in both locations just to switch things up!

★ **Style:** Treehouses and bungalows on the river
💰 **Budget:** $$
📍 **Where:** Tucked off the main street - 5 minute walk

BOOK HERE

Khao Sok Silver Cliff Resort

If you want to be treated like a VIP princess without spending a royal amount of cash, come to Khao Sok Silver Cliff Resort where you will be spoiled and loved by the owners and staff.

Located on the river surrounded by limestone cliffs, here's an extra chance to unplug. Come for solitude in a little hut in the jungle where you can stroll through the garden, wade in the river and dine at the restaurant which has fantastic curries! The owners will take care of you like a daughter! The only catch is that you need a scooter to access the town - otherwise it's about a 40-minute walk on foot. I suggest you stay here for the beginning of your trip & the bungalow package, then move to a more walkable location on your last night or two.

★ *Style:* Private Bungalows
💵 *Budget:* $
📍 *Where:* In the forest on the river under a cliff!

BOOK HERE

. . . .

Coco Hostel

The most popular hostel in Khao Sok and the best place to book your tours! They've got river rafting, canoeing, overnight bungalows and more - and I love that they specify that these trips are for solo travelers. That means you'll likely be on these tours with other travelers from your hostel, especially if you can campaign for some group fun amongst your dorm mates. Even if you don't stay here, book your tours here.

★ *Style:* Dorms
💵 *Budget:* $
📍 *Where:* Khao Sok Street

BOOK HERE

. . . .

Chillax Hostel

Wow the private rooms here have the most amazing views - and on a budget! This hostel is very clean and you won't find many bugs around here! So if you were worried about jungle critters, stay here. Also, the staff at Chillax are so helpful if you feel like you're getting a high-end concierge service included as the owner speaks amazing English!

Chillax also organized my transport from Khao Sok to Krabi - they offered the best deal I could find in Khao Sok and I wasn't even staying here. It's just in their nature to take care of travelers.

★**Style:** Private rooms and dorms

📖**Budget:** $

📍**Where:** Khao Sok Street

BOOK HERE

Where to Eat in Khao Sok

———

I recommend you use my picks as a starting point but as you wander the main road, follow your stomach...

♥ **Pawn's Restaurant -** Thai Food that you crave

♥ **Nongsaw Thai Food -** Very authentic Thai food with flavors and textures that are fantastic if you're open minded.

♥ **Khao Sok Rasta -** Cozy seating on the ground with fantastic soups and curries

♥ **Chao Italian Pizza -** Wood fired oven pizza in the jungle plus carafes of wine!

♥ **NumNgern Coffee & Restaurant -** Vegan and vegetarians, rejoice!

♥ **Jumanji Bar -** A mystical little bar tucked away in a Alice-in-Wonderland garden

The Ultimate Khao Sok Itinerary

DAY 1: ARRIVE

○ Arrive in Khao Sok and check into Hotel #1.

○ Grab a bite to eat and then discuss your tours with the hotel

○ Book the following:

→ A river floating adventure

→ The night safari

→ and just one night at the floating bungalows (not the 2-night package)

○ Wander the town and unplug.

DAY 2: TOUR DAY

○ Float the river and go on the Night Safari

○ Keep your Night Safari ticket which you can use for tomorrow's bungalows.

○ Pack a mini-bag for tomorrow - and plan to leave the rest of your stuff at the hotel.

DAY 3: OVERNIGHT BUNGALOWS

Best day of your life!

○ A van will pick you up in the morning and take you to the lake. You'll meet other travelers that will become your summer camp buddies and you'll share a jaw-droppingly beautiful longtail boat ride to your bungalows.

○ Throw your bags down and then head back out with the crew for a wild adventure either swimming through caves or hiking to a viewpoint.

○ Alternatively, you can do what I did: Kayak around the lake and visit the fisherman's tiny shop where you can buy beer and snacks (they were so surprised to see me).

○ Spend the rest of the day jumping in the lake from your bungalows, eating dinner with the group and having a couple beers under the stars.

DAY 4: YOU HAVE TWO OPTIONS

○ Wake up early for a morning safari by boat to spot monkeys in the trees!

Option 1: When you're picked up from the lake, get dropped off at your Hotel #2

Option 2: Pre-organize your direct can transfer to either Krabi or Surat Thani (where you can go to Koh Samui or back to Bangkok).

the rest of your stuff will be in the van that picks you up

DAY 5: KHAO SOK

○ Did you stay in Khao Sok? Good! Changing hotels gives you a totally different experience!

○ Stay for another 2-3 days. Rent a motorbike, get massages, and make new friends.

Pro Tips for Khao Sok

Book as you Go

Don't book all your tours right now. Wait until you get there and book the night before or the day of. You can even do this with the overnight experience at the lake, especially if you're just playing it by ear!

The Trick to Booking Tours

Booking through hostels is cheaper for solo travelers, but booking for more than 1 person is fair at any of the accommodations I've listed. If you're not staying at the hostel, double confirm they can pick you up from your accommodation for free - otherwise it's a pain in the butt to schlep yourself to the hostel or pay more.

Do not join any elephant experiences

I did so much indepth research and whenever I thought I had found an ethical elephant sanctuary, I'd discover that they were just really good at hiding the mistreatment of their elephants. There are more ethical experiences in Chiang Mai, Phuket, and Koh Samui.

Don't take everything with you on the overnight trip

Everyone that got on our boat either had a small day bag with a change of clothes or a dry bag. Pack like you're going camping and leave your electronics & extra things behind. If you're staying at a hostel, you can lock them in a locker and know they're secure. If you're staying at a luxury place like My Jungle House, you can trust them to keep your things safe. I took just my drone, toiletry bag and one change of clothes for the next day - I wore my suit.

Getting Into Khao Sok

12go.asia is going to be where you book everything

FROM BANGKOK - HEAD TO SURAT THANI TOWN

○ **Option 1: The Best Way to Get to Khao Sok -**

Take the sleeper train from Bangkok to Surat Thani Town.

I plan my itineraries in Thailand around the sleeper train! It's such a unique and comfortable experience. It's also a bargain, bundling transportation and accommodation in one.

- ♥ **Book:** Train #167 with Thai Railways in 2nd Class Sleeper AC
- ♥ **Departs Bangkok:** 6:30pm
- ♥ **Arrives in Surat Thani:** 7:48am
- ⊕ **Ticket:** Get your ticket on 12go.asia - book the bottom bunk if possible.

☞ I have a whole blog about the sleeper train including tips and advice at TheSoloGirlsTravelGuide.com.

○ **Option 2: Fly to Surat Thani Airport**

FROM SURAT THANI TO KHAO SOK

You'll need to get in a private taxi or a shared bus/minivan.

○ *Option 1:* Arrange private pick-up via car.

♥ **How to Book:** Try 12go.asia first (they're usually the cheapest around $40 usd) - but the most comfortable ride which guarantees no miscommunications or need for directions is to book with your hotel or with Chillax Hostel for 2,000 baht or less ($60).

⊙ **How long:** 1.5 hours

○ **Option 2: Take a public bus from Surat Thani town** at 8:30am or 10am which costs less than 100 baht (around $7 USD).

♥ **How to Book:** Book on 12go.asia and then make your way to Surat Thani Town.

To get to Surat Thani Town from the airport or the train station, simply get in a taxi and tell them Surat Thani Town. This costs around 140 baht from the train station and 250 baht from the airport.

🏢 **Address:** Suratthani Branch (MAIN OFFICE) is at 293/6-8 Taladmai Road, Amphur Muang, Suratthani

⊙ **How Long:** 3-4 hours (they make some stops along the way).

FROM KRABI

○ **Option 1: Take a Public Bus or Shared Van**

Vans and buses leave all day long from Krabi and will even pick you up at your hotel

⊙ **How Long:** 5 hours

💰 **Budget:** $7-$11 USD

○ **Option 2: Or a Private Car**

A private car costs about $75 and takes 2.5 hours - picking you up and dropping you off door to door

This sounds complicated but it's all part of the fun. If Khao Sok was easy to reach, it wouldn't be hidden!

HOW TO LEAVE KHAO SOK

Remember, 12go.asia will be your lifeline. You can rely on them to get you where you need to go - but here's a sneak peek.

TO KRABI:

○ **Public Transfer** - There is a bus leaving Khao Sok Bus Terminal 5x a day headed to Krabi for $11 USD / 400-450 baht - In reality, it takes 3-5 hours depending on how many tops they make…and it will be a mystery.

○ **Private Transfer** - We paid $75 USD / 2,700 baht with a small car that we organized with Chillax Hostel - it took 2.5 hours. Prices vary depending on where you book.

TO SURAT THANI:

○ **Public Transport** - There is a mini van 2x a day in the early morning hours of 6:30am and 8am that heads to Surat Thani town. From there, you'll find services to transfer you to the boats, the airport or the train station. This is a 2.5 hour minivan that costs $7 USD

○ **Private Transfer** - Around $60 USD / 2,000 baht and it takes 1.5-2 hours

Hey, I love Khao Sok so much - so please tag me in your videos and photos so I can follow your adventure @sologirlstravelguide

And please send me your tips and recommendations - I love learning through you.

BONUS!

A Bit of
Khao Sok History

Cheow Lan Lake actually used to be a small town. That small town was dammed and flooded to become what is now an electricity producing dam, a protected wildlife sanctuary and home to fresh fish farms where local fishermen live. Here's the condensed version of how it happened according to KhaoSok.com:

○**1944:** A deadly pandemic swept through the region killing most of its inhabitants and encouraging the rest to move away. The village became known as "Ban Sop" or "Village of the Dead" which remained mostly uninhabited by humans for decades. This allowed the natural world to run wild. Animals, flora and fauna thrived.

○**1971:** A communist regime took over the dense forests as their territory to hide and operate guerilla warfare. Consequently, the land was protected from the logging & mining industry which would have surely wiped out the forest and elimited its biodiversity.

○**1982:** Occupation ended and The National Park Division of Thailand moved in. They convinced small villages to move to nearby land so they could create a sustainable energy-producing dam.

○**1987:** The dam was created, flooding the region and creating the beautiful Cheow Larn Lake and establishing a protected territory for wildlife to thrive. Lots of animals died in the process but the populations are now being restored.

CHAPTER FOUR

Phuket

BEST FOR:

Just keep reading...

PHUKET ··········

CHAPTER FOUR

Phuket

Listen babe, I'm going to do you a favor and advise you to skip Phuket all together.

If you must go to Phuket (like you have a flight out of here), then you need to get my other Thailand book, "Thailand Islands and Beaches."

In this book, I include a Phuket survival guide that shows you how to strategically use Phuket as your base, while finding hidden gems and avoiding the scams.

And ya know what…I make Phuket pretty fun. But would I recommend my little sister to spend her trip here? Not at all.

THE TRUTH ABOUT PHUKET...

Phuket is a convenient place to fly into to quickly access islands like Koh Phi Phi and Koh Lanta or Khao Lak - but that's about it.

Actually, staying in Phuket…don't do it.

15 years ago, Phuket was gorgeous. Today, Phuket is one big tourist trap full of crowded beaches and disappointment. Don't believe the Instagram lies.

Full of sex tourism, outrageous prices, and a taxi mafia with a monopoly on transportation (yes, that's a thing) – your vacation here winds up being 2x as expensive and 3x as stressful. Not to mention, Phuket has the highest rate of drownings in the country and almost zero safety standards on the water.

The actual Thailand you're dreaming of, with white sand beaches and turquoise water, is nearby on islands like Koh Phi Phi or peninsulas like Railay Beach.

So, what do you do if you've already booked your flights to Phuket before reading this book? Or still plan on booking flights directly to Phuket for convenience?

- Stay in Phuket Old Town at Baan Suwantawe Hotel.
- Explore Old Town on foot.
- The airport bus leaves from across the street starting at 6am.

THAE JIRAPON

STAYING MORE THAN ONE NIGHT?

•———————•

Get my Thailand Islands and Beaches guide book.

Yep, I have another Thailand book that is dedicated to all the islands and beaches that are off the beaten path. This book also includes a Phuket Survival Guide…which actually makes Phuket pretty fun.

If you don't have my guidebook, get off Phuket immediately.

After you've survived Phuket…immediately head to the neighboring province of Krabi, Koh Lanta or Koh Phi Phi where you can snorkel, kayak, and swim to your heart's content for half the price.

•———————•

Now, let's get to THOSE chapters. Way more fun!

CHAPTER FIVE

Krabi & Ao Nang Beach

BEST FOR:

An easy-to-get-to beach town with beautiful beaches

DAYS NEEDED:

2-3 days

Krabi & Ao Nang Beach

Just a quick 1-hour flight from Bangkok and a 2-hour flight from Chiang Mai, Krabi Town is where your southern adventures will likely begin and/or end. This is a small walkable beach town with great food, lots of little roadside shopping and a hidden beach that I recommend you go find!

But honestly, the main reason you come to Krabi is to go to Railay Beach, which you'll fall in love with in Chapter 5. You'll touch down in Krabi airport, take a bus or taxi to Ao Nang Beach and catch a longtail boat over to Railay. I'll explain this later.

If you have extra time in your itinerary, however, I usually like to spend one night in Ao Nang before heading to Railay.

Other reasons to stay in Ao Nang:

○ Late flight into Krabi. Stay in Ao Nang for a night, explore Ao Nang for the morning, and head to Railay around noon.

○ Have an early flight out of Krabi. Don't get stuck on Railay. It's best to come to Ao Nang or Krabi town the night before your flight.

○ After Ao Nang Beach, you head to Railay Beach.

○ After Railay beach, you can head to Koh Phi Phi, Koh Lanta, or Phuket - or you can go back towards Krabi Airport. This zone is one of the best travel hubs around - there is no reason to skip it!

AREA BREAKDOWN OF KRABI

❶ Krabi Town

A main hub for transportation and commerce, Krabi Town offers a peek into local life with cheap street food and bustling restaurants filled with Thais. Take your pick of affordable guest houses near the bus station or along the river. Your money goes far in this neck of the woods. To get to the beach from here, you'll need to take some form of transportation – Songthaews are a good option.

❷ Ao Nang Beach

The main tourist area, Ao Nang Beach is highlighted by one very long road in an 'L-Shape' that stretches up down the hill from town and then curves along the beach. The entirety of this massive road is lined with hostels, bars, restaurants, tourist desks and of course, tons of shopping where you can buy swimsuits, sun glasses, snorkel gear and more.

❸ Nopparat Thara Beach

The beach just north of Ao Nang Beach. It's been very over-developed to cater to Chinese tourists, and feels very western and stringent. But it has good shopping and if you have time to kill, it is an interesting walk or scooter ride adventure.

How To Move Around Krabi

Walk

Krabi Town, Ao Nang, and Railay/Tonsai are all walkable! You could go your whole trip and not take any public transportation if you bring the right pair of shoes and some sunscreen.

Songthaews

Just like in the rest of Thailand, you can flag down a Songthaew, tell them where you're going, and jump in the back. Press the little buzzer button if you want to hop off early. Most Songthaew rides in Krabi town will cost 20 baht.

Longtail Boats

You'll be taking a longtail boat over to Railay and you can even take a longtail boat over to Pai Plong Beach if you don't feel like walking up and down the monkey stairs.

"Wandering re-establishes the original harmony which

once existed between man and the universe."

- ANOTOLE FRANCE

Where to Stay in Krabi Province

Krabi Province is quite big and includes Krabi Town, Ao Nang Beach, Railay Beach, and Tonsai. Got all that? Let's break it down…

AO NANG BEACH ACCOMMODATION

Ao Nang is the main beach on the mainland. Staying here means that you can shop to your heart's content and go on island hopping tours during the day, then hit up some restaurants and bars with live music at night.

Phra Nang Inn by Vacation Village

You came here for the beach, right? Phra Nang Inn puts you 30-seconds from the sand without breaking the bank. Wake up and eat breakfast with views of palm trees and the ocean. When you're ready for an adventure, you're just steps from all the tourist kiosks offering every boat tour imaginable - including the longtail boat to Railay. After your day in the sun, come back and swim in the jungle-esque pool surrounded by lush greenery. **PRO TIP!** This is where I choose to stay when I come to Ao Nang, before I head over to Railay. I usually stay here if my flight gets in later than 4pm. For the best view, ask for room #2469 when you book

HEADS UP! You can hear music from nearby bars til about midnight - but it's not a huge bother.

💵 *Budget:* $$

🏨 *Address:* 119 Moo 2 Aonang

BOOK HERE

The L Resort Krabi

You know what I love more than a private pool villa? A room with pool-access where you can jump from your bed into the pool! The little balcony provides the best place for people watching and chilling out with a book (this book). Bonus: You're right across the street from Ao Nang Beach and all the best shopping and restaurants!

💸 *Budget:* $$$
🏨 *Address:* 31 Moo 2

BOOK HERE

Ban Sainai Resort - SHA Extra Plus

Private bungalows and a big pool nestled amongst a lush tropical garden with friendly service, fabulous breakfast and free shuttles to the beach…this is exactly what you imagined when you pictured coming to Thailand. Tucked away on a side-street off the main drag, you're just a 15-minute walk from the action. Afterwards, you can come back to your little slice of paradise, listen to the crickets and watch the stars.

💸 *Budget:* $$$
🏨 *Address:* 550 Moo 2, Soi Ao Nang 11/1

BOOK HERE

Whalecome Resort

The most adorable, female-friendly guesthouse in Ao Nang! If you're on a budget and aren't really the "dorm room" type of girl - Whalecome Aonang offers a happy medium of privacy and price. This is a boutique resort tucked into the trees right behind the main road in Aonang. Each room has its own little balcony and there's a pool! Set off on foot for about 10-15 minutes and you'll reach the beach. Come back to solitude in your simple, but pleasant room to relax. This is the best bang for your buck, if you ask me! Bonus: It's next to my favorite restaurant called Family Ao Nang.

💸 *Budget:* $$
🏨 *Address:* Ao Nang

BOOK HERE

K Bunk

The most social hostel ever with friendship practically built-in to your experience! You'll meet tons of travelers from all over the world. Together you will go on pub crawls, play drinking games, go on beach excursions and boat tours… then bond over how bad your hangover is the morning after. This hostel is located at the very top of the road that leads down to the beach – you can't walk to the beach, but K Bunk will take care of that with free beach transfers.

🛥 *Budget:* $
🛏 *Address:* 376/41 Ao Nang

BOOK HERE

KRABI TOWN ACCOMMODATION

Closer to the airport than the beach, Krabi Town offers a taste of authentic Thai culture with riverside hotels, night markets, temples, and motorbike adventures.

Staying in Krabi Town is a fun way to spend your last (or first) day or two.

The Brown Hotel

After a week of living in your bathing suit, sometimes you just want to clean up, wash your hair, and watch the news. The Brown Hotel is the perfect place to do that before you head to the airport the next day. You can even add a last dose of adventure into your itinerary as this hotel is within walking distance to the night market and a short ride away from Tiger Cave Temple. Going to Koh Lanta next? This is also a convenient spot for smooth transport.

🛥 *Budget:* $
🛏 *Address:* 6 Maharaj Soi.2 Rd., Paknam, Mueang

BOOK HERE

Things to Do in Krabi

The Krabi Province, including Ao Nang Beach, Railay Beach and Tonsai Beach, is quite compact. Any tour that you want to go on can be reached from any of the above locations. It doesn't matter where you stay- there is a long-tail boat waiting to take you to your destination. So let's get into it...

Monkey Path to Coast Beach Club

Walk to the south end of Ao Nang Beach, through The Last Fisherman's Bar and you'll see a set of rickety wooden stairs going into the jungle. Climb em'. This path takes you through the jungle with some interesting viewpoints and monkeys in the trees. Eventually the stairs will start climbing down and let out at Pai Plong Beach. **FYI:** The stairs to get down here are a workout! And require you to watch your step.

Relax and Swim at Pai Plong Beach

A beautiful beach that is hidden from the crowds of tourists over at Ao Nang! Pai Plong Beach is a small, stunning beach with amazing sunsets, a 5-star hotel and a beach club called the Coast Club! You can go and order a drink at the Coast Club, get cozy and take your time enjoying the beach! Or come with your own bottles of water and snacks, put a towel down and spend your day running in and out of the water.

Walk to Nopparat Thara Beach

The beach itself isn't anything spectacular and the area mostly caters to Chinese tourists. But there are two gems on this beach: Frog Bar which is a beachfront hut with cold beers and Punjab palace which is owned by a sweet Indian family that has some of the cheapest food and drink prices around. The walk is easy and scenic.

Krabi Town Walking Street

The mecca of shopping, culture, eating, and drinking, Krabi Town Walking Street should not be overlooked! This is your chance to peruse over 50 stalls selling handmade treasures like chic leather purses, sparkly sandals, and cheesy 'Krabi' t-shirts and tank tops. Eat while you shop with stall after stall of sweet and savory Thai treats. Ps. This market is a good excuse to stay in Krabi Town for one night if you have the time.

⊙ **Open:** Friday - Sunday from 5:30pm – 10pm

♀ **Where:** Soi Maharaj 8 - behind Vogue Department Store

↻ **How to Get There:** From Ao Nang... The cheapest way is to flag down a songthaew, ask if they're going to Krabi Town Walking Street (best if you show them on GoogleMaps) and join the ride; after a few zig zag stops, they'll eventually drop you at the market. This is how you'll return, as well. The other way is by tuk tuk.

Watch a Muay Thai Fight

Blood, sweat and beer – that's what you can expect with a night at the matches. Sometimes children fight and sometimes adults fight. What's important to remember is that Muay Thai is a respected sport, not some barbaric death match. Locals come to bet on matches and fighters have been training for months to get their turn in the ring! Some nights, the crowds are wild and some nights you practically get the whole show to yourself. Don't expect a Las Vegas show, but a wild view into Thai Culture!

💸 **Budget:** Ringside for 1,800 baht OR Open Stadium seating for 1,200 baht. They both give you a great show – just stick with your budget.

🎟 **Tickets:** You can buy tickets at the stadium on fight night, from a tour office or possibly, from your hotel.

Best Tours in Krabi

Mangrove & Cave Kayaking Tour

Explore a maze of mangroves, caves, and jungle via kayak! The laziest way to get into nature and sightsee, these guided tours feel super relaxed as you glide over still water channels with barely any current at all- just a little paddle navigation required. If ever there was a time to try kayaking for the first time- this is it, sister! The mangrove tours are half-day tours that include hotel transfers, snacks, and some swimming! The water is super still, so if ever there was a time to try kayaking for the first time- this is it, sister! If you're in the mood for a crazier adventure, there are full-day tours over slightly more challenging routes, as well. Check out Sea-Kayak Krabi or Krabi Cavemen for options!

💸 **How Much:** Tours from $30 USD / 1000 baht   **Book here:**

Ya's Thai Cookery School Class

While you'll find tons of fabulous cooking schools in Krabi – this is the cooking class that I took and loved. You'll start your day at the market shopping for fresh ingredients to whip up 6 Thai dishes. The chef, Ya, speaks English and has a great sense of humor – so don't worry about being a master chef! Just have fun. After every course is cooked, you'll sit down to eat! When the class is over, you'll go home with a recipe book and perhaps the best souvenir ever: the skills to cook Thai food at home. Going alone or with a friend? This is a great way to meet new people as each class is an intimate group of 4-6 people.

💸 **How Much:** $60 USD / 2000 baht

Adventures with Scooters

You'll see tours for the Emerald Pool and Hot Springs…which just ends up packing these pools with tourists and totally takes away from the magic. The best way to go here is either by yourself on a motorbike or by hiring a tuk tuk driver to take you before or after the tours get there.

The Emerald Pool

The Emerald Pool is this gorgeous blue, almost glowing, natural spring in the middle of the jungle! The water is cool and crystal clear with little streams and mini pools surrounding it– perfect for swimming! To reach the Emerald Pool, you'll stroll along a jungle path leading to smaller pools and the Blue Pool (closed May-October) scattered along the way. Stop and swim wherever you please.

The trick to enjoying the Emerald Pool is to go in the morning before the crowd! Drive yourself on a motorbike or hire a tuk tuk driver to take you so that you can avoid the organized van tour times that make the Emerald Pool feel like a public pool.

🏷 **Budget:** 30 baht
🕗 **Open:** 8:00am – 5:00pm

Krabi Hot Springs

Riiiiight nearby The Emerald Pool you can find these natural hot springs that reach up to 95-107 F (35-42 C). Just like the Emerald Pool, the hot springs are surrounded by forest with hot little pools and waterfalls where you can climb, swim, and soak. There is also a cool river at the base of the hot springs where you can take a refreshing dip at the end of your natural spa day!

To get there on your own, literally just plug "Krabi Hot Springs" into the GPS and you're all set. Once you reach the parking lot, you go through a gate and pay a small entrance fee. Follow the gray brick path where you'll pass the first hot spring – but this one looks more like a sparkly swimming pool with concrete bottom.

Hike Tab Kak Hang Nak Hill Nature Trail

Half scooter and half feet – this is a bucket list adventure for my girls who like to get sweaty. Tab Kak Hang Nak Hill Nature Trail is a true hike through the jungle on a moderately steep 2.5-mile path. The paths are clearly marked to keep you on track as you make your way over little bridges, under tall jungle canopy and on top of pure earth, rocks, and roots at your feet.

During the two to three-hour trek, you will come across stunning vistas and viewpoints of rolling mountains and crystal blue shores. Along the way, you'll find small natural waterfalls and swimming holes. Then at the very top, you'll reach the 360-degree viewpoint – called Hang Na Cape - that makes the whole butt-burning hike worth it.

↻ **How to Get There:** Drive an hour out of Krabi Town to Khao Ngon Nak National Park. At the entrance of the park, you'll find a little parking lot next to the trail entrance. At the trail entrance, there will be a big map of the trail, the paths, and the viewpoints that you want to look out for along the way. **PRO TIP!** Start in the morning and check the weather! You don't want to hike in a

Tiger Cave Temple

What does 1,237 steps up a Thai mountain get you? A 360 degree panoramic view of Krabi Town along with a gorgeous Buddhist Temple that glistens in the sun! This Buddhist Temple dates back to 1975, founded by monk looking to meditate in peace….who instead found a cave full of tigers. This spot became sacred for the monks, who adorned the mountain with golden Buddhist statues and shrines. Plan to spend 1 hour hiking and 30 minutes wandering…and 5 minutes to buy some bananas and feed the monkeys.

⊙ **Open:** All day
♥ **Where:** 3km from Krabi Town
↻ **How to Get There:** Rent a motorbike for ~$5 and follow the signs OR hire a tuk tuk driver to take you up.

PRO TIP: Dress respectfully by covering your shoulders and knees.

Don't want to scooter it?

Go on the Tiger Cave and Hot Springs Tour. ☞

Shopping in Krabi

Ao Nang Road

The main road that leads outlines Ao Nang Beach and stretches up towards Krabi Town is filled with shops and stalls selling everything under the sun! Cute bags, dresses, jewelry, oils, soaps – you name it. There is also beach gear like snorkels and Dry Bags to keep your phone safe from sand and water. Just be sure to haggle! You can always get a cheaper price.

Krabi Town Walking Street Market

There's more than just food at the night market here! Browse handmade treasures like chic leather purses, sparkly sandals, and cheesy 'Krabi' t-shirts and tank tops. Eat while you shop with stall after stall of sweet and savory Thai treats.

⊙ **Open:** Friday - Sunday from 5:30pm – 10pm
♥ **Where:** Soi Maharaj 8 - behind Vogue Department Store

♥ Check out my Thailand Packing Guide at
TheSoloGirlsTravelGuide.com

Where to Eat in Krabi

AO NANG BEACH

Family Aonang

Easily my favorite restaurant in Ao Nang! Whenever I visit, I eat 50% of my meals at Family. My favorite dish? The Kua Kling chicken fried in hot southern chili paste. It's spicy! You're going to need rice on the side and a big cold beer to go with it. Not into spicy? Order literally anything your mouth desires. This is a family owned restaurant (duh) who cooks for you like you're in their family home. So yum.

⊙ **Open:** 10am – 10:30pm
♥ **Where:** Ao Nang - same street as WhaleCome

Cafe 8.98

Amazing breakfast and coffee. Western style but also western prices. If you're on a budget, skip it. Chia mango pudding bowl for 120 thb ($5 usd) or a smoothie bowl for 240 tho ($7 usd) or a smoked salmon and avocado omelet for 240 thb ($7 usd). The WiFi is strong. There are definitely cheaper options out there but if you want clean, fresh food in a clean and bright space right on the main road - this is your spot! Fresh pressed juices

⊙ **Open:** 7am-11pm
🏠 **Address:** 143/7-8, Ao Nang
↻ **How to Get There:** 5-minutes up Ao Nang Road on the left

RCA Entertainment

The key to finding the best cheap food is to go where ugly men go to find "intimate company" for the night. Yep, old men love good food and cheap prices. You get both here plus some fantastic people watching. I, personally, enjoy the red light districts in Thailand because no men are there to hit on me. I'm not the flavor they're craving, you know what I mean?

If you're in the mood for something sweet, go to one of the food stalls selling roti and order a chocolate banana roti.

⊘ *Best Time to Come:* Dinner - Late Night
♥ *Where:* Across from Cafe 8.98. Look for "Street food stalls" on GoogleMaps

The Last Fisherman Bar

Eat dinner with your toes in the sand right next to the crashing waves! The Last Fisherman Bar is a casual restaurant underneath the trees that brings in freshly-caught seafood every day! Food is extremely well-priced considering the million-dollar ocean front view. Expect dishes to be anywhere from 200 baht – 800 baht made with fresh ingredients. Cocktails start at 180 baht - a small price to pay to watch the sun set in Thailand.

⊘ *Open:* 10am – 11pm
♥ *Where:* Ao Nang Beachfront
↻ *How to Get There:* Where the main road first hits Ao Nang beach, go left down the footpath until you cross under a sign that says The Last Fisherman Bar.

Night Market Place

A small yet lively night market with cheap food and lots to look at! Come for dinner where you can hop from stall to stall collecting fresh seafood on skewers, stir fried noodles, grilled fish, coconut ice cream and more. This market is just a short walk from the beach and a fun little stroll past shops and tiny markets. It's a safe and easy adventure, perfect for solo travelers.

⊙ *Open:* Daily 5pm - 10pm

ↄ *How to Get There:* Follow the main road along the beach which will start winding up to the right

♥ *GoogleMaps:* Night Market Place

KRABI TOWN

Krabi Night Market

Street food is calling! For 30-100 baht per, you can try every Thai dish under the sun alongside southern Muslim curries and Chinese wok dishes. There are plenty of tables and chairs mixed in with stall after stall of fresh flavors to taste! Plus, street performers!

⊙ *Open:* Daily from 5:30pm – 10pm

♥ *Where:* Krabi Town

ↄ *How to Get There:* Jump in a 20 - 40 baht Songthaew from Ao Nang

Gecko Cabane Restaurant

A cozy Thai restaurant with cheap beer and classic dishes, Gecko Cabane is a great place to pop in for lunch or a laid-back dinner. The staff are fabulously hospitable and attentive – they certainly are not on Thai time here! You can expect friendly service along with Thai dishes that represent what Thai people typically eat on any given day in the South of Thailand. Oh, and don't worry about your food being too spicy- they staff usually ask how spicy you'd like your dish on a 1-10 scale!

⊙ *Open:* Daily 11am-2pm & 5pm-11pm

♥ *Where:* 1/36-37 Soi Ruamjit, Maharat Road, Krabi Town

ↄ *How to Get There:* Walk 10 minutes west of the night market, into town along Soi Ruamjit

Nightlife in Krabi

My biggest tip for nightlife in Krabi is to simply follow the music and neon lights. But there's one place I certainly recommend...

Jojo Reggae Bar

If you're not a huge party girl but you want to sit in some plastic chairs outside a reggae bar next to a mini mart with a 99 bath cocktail - this is your spot. Jojo Reggae Bar is tiny which means whoever else is sitting there, you're talking to. I love that this little booze-hut is just off the main drag which means you get to partake in my favorite drinking hobby: people watching!

⊙ **Open:** Whenever they feel like it
🏛 **Address:** 32/18 4203
📍 **Where:** You can easily walk there, along the main road, from the beach

How to Get into Krabi & Ao Nang

○ Option1: Fly

Krabi's airport is not international, but you can catch a flight here.

→ **Bangkok:** 1.5 hours

→ **Chiang Mai:** 2 hours

→ **Koh Samui:** 1 hour

Depending on where you're coming from, some flights might have you transit through Bangkok.

○ Option 2: Boat

There are tons of islands west of Krabi. Take a boat either to Ao Nang Beach or directly to Railay.

→ **Koh Phi Phi:** 30 minutes

→ **Koh Lanta:** 2.5 hours

→ **Phuket:** 3.5 hours

○ Option3: On Land

Vans, buses and cars can all reach Krabi very easily from all around the country. A taxi is faster than a bus, obviously. The times below are the general average between bus and taxi (depending on traffic).

→ **Phuket:** 2.5 hours

→ **Koh Lanta:** 2 hours

→ **Surat Thani (the eastern island province where you'll find Koh Samui, Koh Phangan and Koh Tao):** 4-5 hours

FROM KRABI INTERNATIONAL AIRPORT

Krabi Airport is tiny. This is great for you! It means less time spent inside the airport and zero chance of getting lost.

The airport is 9 miles from the city center, 24 miles from Ao Nang and 14 miles from Had Yao—and there are a couple different ways to reach your destinations.

Expect to take about 45mins–1 hour to get from the airport to your destination. It sounds like a long ride…but the drive is beautiful!

○ Option 1: Fixed Rate Taxi

There are no metered taxis at Krabi Airport—only fixed rate. Prices can vary but the below prices are a good reference.

♥ Where: You will find taxi booths inside the Arrivals Hall

💶 How Much: (give or take 100 Baht)

Krabi Town: 400 Baht

Ao Nang: 500 Baht

Had Yao: 800 Baht

Railay Pier (boat included): 700 Baht

○ Option 2: Airport Shuttle Bus

♥ Where: You can buy tickets at the same place as the taxi booth inside the Arrivals Hall. Go out of the arrival doors (you'll still be inside the airport) and make a left. You'll see a sign for "Shuttle Bus".

💶 How Much:

Krabi Town: 100 Baht

Ao Nang: 150 Baht

☉ When: The Shuttle Bus leaves 8–10 times between 8am–8pm (so almost once per hour). Once you get your ticket, you'll go outside of the airport and see a big white bus. Most travelers take this bus so the staff will wrangle you on board.

○ Option 3: Pre-Booked Private Transfers

Book ahead of time with YourKrabi.com and have a car or minivan waiting to take you to your hotel.

💸 *How Much:*

Hotels in Krabi Town: minivan 800 Baht

Hotels in the Ao Nang: minivan 800 Baht

Hotels in Koh Lanta: minivan 2,500–2,800 Baht, depending on where on the island you are staying.

○ Option 4: Songthaews to Krabi Town

📍 *Where:* Walk about 400 meters to the main road and flag down a public Songthaew.

💸 *How Much:*

Krabi Town: 30–50 Baht

🕐 *When:* 6am–11pm (roughly)

FROM KRABI BUS STATION

○ Option 1: Songthaews to Krabi Town

📍 *Where:* You'll see brown and white Songthaews once you step off the bus. They each go in different directions—so show them where you hotel is located on a map and one or the other will let you know if they go your route.

💸 *How Much:*

Krabi Town: 20 Baht

Ao Nang: 60 Baht (White Songthaew)

🕐 *When:* All bus hours

○ Option 2: Metered Taxi

📍 *Where:* You'll see taxis once you step off the bus.

💸 *How Much:* Krabi Town: roughly 100 Baht

Ao Nang: roughly 150 Baht

Anywhere else you'd like to go, just make sure they run the meter.

🕐 *When:* All hours that buses arrive

CHAPTER SIX

Railay

BEST FOR:

Living barefoot in your bathing suit, feeling safe as you bar hop
and beach hop.

DAYS NEEDED:

2-3 days

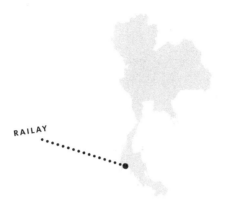

RAILAY

CHAPTER SIX

Railay

I never come to Thailand without planning at least a few days on Railay. Railay is not an island, it's actually a peninsula jetting off from Ao Nang Beach, only accessible by boat! So once you're here, you're here. You take your shoes off before your longtail boat even hits the sand, and they don't go back on your feet until you leave.

This is the kind of place where you lose track of time and space. The kind of place where your time is segmented by your meals and not your watch. You'll often put your sunscreen on and throw everything you have into a tote bag and leave your hotel - not to return until after dark. It's not that you're doing anything particularly time-consuming; you're just going with the flow bouncing from beach to bar. Railay is its own little universe and a total mind reset.

Once you're here, you can plan on a budget or throw cash around like Oprah. Live it up in fancy resorts or party barefoot with local expats – you've got all the options! Most attractive about Railay, however, are the skyscraper islands that tower over warm blue water and powdery-soft sand beaches like a scene out of Avatar. Bring your phone ready to take pictures…just don't let the monkeys steal it out of your purse when you're done.

BEACH BREAKDOWN:

Your whole world will revolve between these for beaches:

① Railay West

This is the main beach where most long tail boats dock – letting you off into sandy paradise. Swim, tan & play here.

② Tonsai Beach

Head to the very north of Railay West and get ready for a climb up the rocks, through a marked path and down to Tonsai Beach on the other side where you'll step into hippie paradise!

③ Phra Nang Cave Beach

Secluded and insanely beautiful, this is the beach you came to Thailand to see! You can easily walk here via the concrete path on Railay East. Bring some snacks and drinks and spend the afternoon here.

❹ Railay East

Where the party happens! Railay East is not really a beach, more of a cove with high and low tides, highlighted by a concrete path that is lined with hotels, restaurants and bars. In the center of the path is the boat pier in the center, Phra Nang Cave Beach is to the very right and party central with restaurants and bars is to the left.

All of these beaches are within leisurely strolling distance to each other.

Are you in love yet?

You will be by the end of this chapter…

How to Get to Railay

___

COMING FROM AO NANG?

Take a Longtail Boat

These classic Thai Longtail boats are waiting at practically every beach to take you on a day tour, to the islands, back to the mainland, etc. Consider them private water taxis.

From Ao Nang to Railay (and vice versa), tickets are 100 baht per person. In Ao Nang, there is a bright yellow kiosk at the bottom of the hill next to the beach where you can buy your ticket.

The boats wait for 8 people to buy a ticket to depart – sometimes you can wait 5 minutes and sometimes 20 minutes. Want to rent the whole boat and get going? 800 baht will get you a private ride to Ao Nang (good idea for photoshoots).

NOTE: If you're getting in late, stay in Ao Nang Beach – water taxis to Railay Beach are scarce after 8pm (particularly in low season).

You will get dropped off on Railay West beach and then you'll walk to your accommodation.

COMING FROM KRABI TOWN OR
ANOTHER TOWN WITH A PRIVATE CAR?

Get dropped at Ao Nammao Pier, it's a more convenient location and boats leave often.

COMING FROM KOH PHI PHI, PHUKET OR KOH LANTA?

Head to a local tour desk and get a boat that will drop you directly here, not stopping in Krabi.

PRO TIP!

I made a YouTube video that shows you what that journey looks like.

Watch it here ☞

Ps. Don't forget to susbscribe to the channel for more Solo Girl Travel Guide adventures!

TRAVEL NOTES:

....

....

....

....

....

Where to Stay in Railay

The beaches on the peninsula, both Railay and Tonsai, offer access to pristine beaches and islands, as well as rock climbing, kayaking, and a plethora of beach bars and restaurants.

Just remember, Tonsai is tucked away from Railay. To get to Tonsai from Krabi, just take a boat. To get to Tonsai from Railay, you'll climb through a rock tunnel at the top of Railay West, but only when the tide is low. When the tide is high, you will have a long-tail boat zip you over.

Want social vibes? Stay on Railay.

Want alone time? Stay on Tonsai.

Or do both.

Avatar Railay

A 4-star resort with 2-star prices? Yes, please. Avatar is by far one of my favorite hotels in all of Thailand and where I stay every time I come to Railay. The pool-access room is incredible! You get a private balcony with stairs leading into the pool and your own cabana bed. If you don't mind spending a little extra... you can upgrade to a villa with a private pool villa – if you book early, that is. Step outside of the hotel and you're on the concrete path that takes you to Railay East nightlife and Phra Nang Cave Beach. Ugh, this place is seriously paradise... but the breakfast sucks. Really, don't even bother.

💸 **Budget:** $$
📍**Where:** East Railay Beach

BOOK HERE

Rayavadee

📷 BOOKING.COM

Excuse my language by holy shit. Rayavadee Resort would easily cost 3x the price back home…but because it's Thailand, you get to melt into the sexiest 5-star resort in Krabi without going bankrupt. Each cottage is surrounded by absolute nature! The pool is breathtaking, the food is to die for and you will be treated like the queen that you are! Worth every damn penny! Pro Tip: Make sure to make a dinner reservation at The Grotto, Rayavadee's incredible rocky restaurant.

💸 **Budget:** $$$$

📍 **Where:** Railay East

BOOK HERE

• •

Railay Bay Resort

Get the One-Bedroom Cottage with Cool-Water Spa Bath or the One Bedroom Luxury Pool Villa. Or nothing at all. This resort is idyllic, located right on the beach where you can watch the longtail boats putter in and out. It's not the newest hotel but the views from the pool, lounge chairs and breakfast table are iconic.

BOOK HERE

💸 **Budget:** $$$

📍 **Where:** Railay Beach

Blanco Hideout Hostel

THE hostel to stay in on Railay (really, it's the only one). Check in, throw your bags down, and go exploring on foot! You're 5-minutes from Phra Nang Cave Beach and right next to the best bars and restaurants. The hostel does a pub crawl three times a week (Monday, Wednesday and Friday) with a 2-hour open-bar at Blanco where you can mingle with other travelers. Plus, there's a big pool overlooking the water next to a little lounging deck with amazing views. What more do you need?

💸 *Budget:* $
📍 *Where:* Railay East

BOOK HERE

Chill Out Bar & Bungalow

No shoes, no bra, no problem. Chill Out Bar is an oasis away from the tourists and away from civilization where you never know what time it is...and it doesn't even matter. Forget your troubles as you take a kayak out for a spin, play a card game with strangers, or learn to rock climb cause YOLO. Minimalistic and simplistic – hit the reset button on life, babe.

💸 *Budget:* $
📍 *Where:* Tonsai Beach

BOOK HERE

Tinidee Hideaway Tonsai Beach Krabi

Hostel or private bungalow? Take your pick - both have incredible ocean views and are surrounded by pure nature. While this beach isn't great for swimming, you can rent kayaks or paddle boards, get a massage or play board games with fellow travelers. Explore the backstreets of Tonsai or walk over to Railay for the day. Or don't. Just stay in your little piece of paradise the whole time.

💸 *Budget:* $
📍 *Where:* Tonsai Bay

BOOK HERE

Things to Do in Railay

Advice: Any time you want to do a tour or activity, go to Army Tours near Coffee Station. This is the most honest tour desk on Railay. Need advice or information? Just come and ask here! Best prices, no scams.

Krabi Sunset Cruise

📷 KRABI SUNRISE CRUISE

The best day you'll have in Krabi…and for many girls, the best day you'll have in Thailand – this 5-island Sunset Cruise is your one-stop-shop to make new friends, snorkel with colorful fish, jump off the rooftop of a pirate ship, kayak or paddle board while the sun sets, and swim with glow-in-the-dark bioluminescent plankton in pitch black water.

Or…don't do any of that. You can just chill on the rooftop, tanning and drinking beers all day. Do as little or as much as you like. The tour includes pick up from Ao Nang or Railay AND a really yummy Thai dinner – suitable for both carnivores and vegetarians. This is a day you'll never forget.

Pro Tip: Not a confident swimmer? This is the best tour for you. Michael, the cute Aussie Boat Captain, will drag your ass around using an inflatable tube that you can hold onto while you snorkel safely. He's a freakishly strong swimmer and there is also a crew of Thai guys who can help you in and out of the water.

You can get picked up in Ao Nang or Railay.

🕐 **When:** Everyday 1pm-8pm

Includes dinner, pickup, drop off, snorkel mask, flippers, kayaks, paddle boards, snacks, drinks, and dinner.

Book here ☞

Go on an Island Hopping Tour

Everywhere you look, you'll see the "4 Islands Tour" being offered. This tour takes you to the most desirable Krabi beaches and islands with unspoiled white sand beaches off of nearby islands where you can hop off and snorkel with some spectacular wildlife. The tours are led by Thai people, so there's no social element or informational angle – rather an opportunity to visit some gorgeous sights and take photos that will make all of your friends jealous.

BUT one of the "stops" on this tour is Phra Nang Cave Beach…which you can walk to from Railay. Kind of a joke but you still get a boat ride.

Book here ☞

Explore Phra Nang Cave Beach + Poda Island

You can access one of the most beautiful beaches you've ever seen via an easy, concrete-paved path. Located on the East Side of Railay, as you follow the path you walk underneath some trees – look up! This is where the monkeys live. They're either in the trees or hanging out on the fence!

Once you walk onto the beach, look to the left. There is a penis-shrine fertility temple (yes, you read that right) tucked in a cave. You'll see mothers here praying for their daughters to get pregnant.

Walk onto the beach to the right and there is the magnificent Poda Island! This is one of my favorite photo spots ever! Bring snacks and a beach towel and hang out here all-day long.

PRO TIP! Really, stay here all day. So many people come to Railay thinking that they need to go on an island tour and get off of Railay. But while everyone is away, you get this beach mostly to yourself. Move your beach towel a couple times throughout the day, heading more north each time and get different perspectives of the beach!

Go Rock Climbing on Tonsai Beach

The natural cliff edge on Tonsai is a rock climber's dream. In fact, rock climbers travel near and far just to scale the cliff with gorgeous views of the sand and water below. The rock climbing crew has up-to-date gear and offers lessons for beginners and advanced climbers.

♥ Where: Tonsai Beach
💷 Budget: Starting at $24 USD / 800 baht with Basecamp Tonsai

Climb to the Lagoon

See that sign that says "Do Not Climb" - that's where you climb. It's a sketchy climb so don't do it alone but if you're brave enough and athletic enough to monkey climb up a cliff using a rope to pull you up, you'll be rewarded by a hidden lagoon. My rock climbing friends have done this and loved it but I'm too much of a chicken. If you do this, let me know how it goes...

♥ Where: On the path to Phra Nang Cave Beach on the left

✎ **JOURNAL PROMPT**

What's my favorite memory from my Thailand trip...

....

....

....

....

....

Where to Eat in Railay

Coffee Station

Remember Owl from Winnie the Pooh? As owls do, he lived comfortably in a little wooden nook where his friends gathered for tea and a chat. The same goes for Coffee Station, except instead of tea you have freshly ground Italian coffee prepared right before your eyes. The coffee is strong, there is a book swap station, and the Thai staff who sleep upstairs are some of the friendliest guys you'll meet.

⊙ **Open:** Morning til night
♀ **Where:** Railay – next to Jamaica Bar

Tew Lay Bar

Walk to the very north end of Railay East and you'll find this Instagram-worthy bar and restaurant where you can chill in a bean bag chair overlooking the water. While you wait for your pizza or Thai food feast, have a little photoshoot. There are big birds nests and platforms jetting out over the ocean which make for the perfect photo to make all your friends at home jealous. Ps. This is one of the best breakfast spots on Railay because it's usually empty!

⊙ **Open:** Daily 9am - Midnight
♀ **Where:** The very north end of Railay East - just follow the boardwalk

Railay Family Restaurant

Run, don't walk. Railay Family Restaurant is my #1 restaurant on Railay and it has been for years! The food only gets better and better! The penang curry with shrimp is my go-to but the menu has everything you could dream of including vegetarian options. Amazing for lunch, amazing for dinner.

⊙ **Open:** Daily Lunch til Close
♀ Where: Between Railay Beach and East Railay Beach
🏠 **Address:** 354 Moo 2, Railay Beach

Mangrove Restaurant

The best roti everrrrrrr! It's the perfect balance between doughy, flakey and chewy! Pair that with a massaman curry and you're in Thai food heaven. You can also order the glass noodle chicken larb! It's Alexa-approved, however, I will warn you that not everything on the menu here is great - not even their specials or 50 baht combo meals. But the roti and massaman and the glass noodle chicken larb make this place a must-visit. After that, move along.

⊙ **Best Time to Come:** For lunch
♀ Where: Right across from Family Restaurant

Kohinoor Indian

I was told by a farang who has lived on Railay for years that Kohinoor Indian is the best Indian food in all of Thailand. I didn't believe him…until I tried it for myself. Holy deliciousness. Order any curry but make sure you also order samosas and lassis. Ps. There are plenty of vegetarian and vegan options here.

⊙ **Open:** 11am - 11pm
♀ Where: Just before Family Restaurant

Local

I often see Thais getting takeaway from Local and that's how you know a place is good. That being said, if you want spicy Thai food come here and ask for your food "pet mak" (very spicy). The portions are generous, the prices are reasonable and the flavors are spot on! I recommend ordering the deep fried papaya salad as a starter. For dessert, order the Mango Sticky Rice!

⊙ **Open:** 10am-10pm
♀ Where: By Kohinoor Indian

1 Stop Take Away Shop

The easiest place to pop in and get a quick bite to eat. They've got it all from pizza to kebabs to fresh fruit shakes - all ready to take away back to your hotel or the beach. They've also got a huge menu of sweet treats like Oreo milkshakes!

⊙ *Open:* Breakfast-Dinner
♥ *Where:* East side of Railay Beach

Railay Story Cafe

The place to go for wood fired pizza. It's not life-changing pizza but it is the best thin crust pizza on Railay that only costs around 200-300 baht! These guys also do to-go orders. Stop by, place an order and come back in 20-minutes for your pizza ready to take to your room or the beach for sunset.

⊙ *Open:* 10am-10pm
♥ *Where:* Walking Street

Railay Rapala Rock Wood Resort

Nachos. Burgers. Vegetarian. Vegan. When you're craving something other than Thai food on Railay Beach, this is the place to go. Nestled in the jungle, Rapala is a tranquil experience with yummy food where you can eat in peace with a good book and a cold beer or iced coffee.

⊙ *Open:* 10am-10pm
♥ *Where:* Railay East

BARS & NIGHTLIFE

Let's be real, cocktail hour starts at 3pm over here. Follow these bars in the order that I list them for your own DIY bar hop.

Black Pearl

A super chill reggae bar with live music in the evening. Black Pearl has a trippy aesthetic and stoner atmosphere which is what the Railay nightlife scene is all about. They offer "happy shakes" but I warn you, they can be potent. As your big sister, I just want to tell you to please take it slow and easy especially if you're solo!

⊖ *Best Time to Come:* After dinner - onwards
♥ *Where:* Right on Railay West

Bamboo Bar

…and tattoo shop. What could go wrong? Bamboo Bar is a little hut under an umbrella with some bar stools wrapped around the bar. You're practically forced to talk to your neighbors! The owners, A and Bo, are super friendly and wind up feeling like long-time buddies. They also happen to make some of the best cocktails on the island! Beware: It is so easy to sit here and keep drinking! Just make sure you order at least one water while you're here.

⊖ *Best Time to Come:* 3pm onwards
♥ *Where:* Walk away from Railay West towards Family Restaurant and you'll spot it on your left.

NEXT: Walk over to Railay East for the real party. ll along the boardwalk you'll find little bars that get wilder and wilder the further you go.

Bang Bang Bar

Solo girl approved, Bang Bang bar is a little hole-in-the-wall for stoners. I don't smoke weed but I liked sitting at the tiny bar chatting to Bang Bang the bartender and joining him in saying "Hello friend" to everyone that walked by. He makes great cocktails and even better conversation no matter how stoned or not stoned you are.

🕐 *Open:* 10:30am-Midnight
📍 *Where:* Right before the path spits you out on Railay East

Why Not Bar

Fire show at 8:30pm!

Ps. I've heard rumors that there might be a name change happening soon. If so, look for East Bar.

Last Bar

The biggest party on all of Railay is here! This is where the pub crawl ends so expect the crowd to be a bit younger. Nevertheless, they have Muay Thai fights, fire dancing and all kinds of backpacker shenanigans at Last Bar. It's a good time if you're looking to have a good time.

Railay Pub Crawl

The fastest way to find new friends to drink with is to join a pub crawl! Railay Pub Crawl throws you into an instant social situation for the night - but most of the participants are under 27 years old, if that matters to you. To sign up, just show up at Blanco Hideout Hostel in person the night of. The group meets around the pool.

📍 *Where:* Begins at Blanco Hideout Hostel
🕐 *Open:* Every Thursday and Sunday around 8pm
💰 *Budget:* 450 baht

Includes a pub crawl tank top, a bucket, free shots and discounts on drinks at each bar

Nightlife on Tonsai Beach

The party scene here is definitely happening…but with more of a trippy 60's "hippie" influence, if you catch my drift. There is fire dancing, reggae music, DJs- all of it. If you plan to partake in hippie activities, stay the night at a guest house on Tonsai.

⚠ Which brings me to my next point which I cannot stress enough!

At night, only party on Tonsai Beach if your accommodation is on Tonsai Beach. Once the sun starts to set and the tide comes up, it is extremely difficult to get back to Railay in the dark, especially if you are a bit buzzed or have been partaking in party activities. The safest alternative is to party on Railay East where you can find similar vibes with a more convenient location.

PRO TIPS FOR RAILAY

🦩 Don't Feed the Monkeys!

These guys are cute but they have sharp teeth and they will steal your stuff!

🦩 Don't Leave Things on your Balcony

They monkeys will steal your stuff! At many resorts, like Avatar, there are two groups of Langur monkeys and Macquaces that come every day and they are greedy.

🦩 What to Do with Your Purse While You're Swimming

You don't hear of people stealing things from the beach often but this is a frequently asked question so here is the answer! Leave your things on the beach underneath your towel and keep an eye on your stuff while swimming. Monkeys are the biggest threat but not a common one on these beaches.

READY TO LEAVE RAILAY?

On the next page I give you the rundown on how to get to your next destination...

Let's go! ☞

To Krabi

To Ao Nang from Railay: You want to take a longtail boat leaving from Railay West. Get your ticket at Army Tour the same day or day before for 100 baht.

To the Airport from Railay

You have two options.

○ **The Cheapest/Slowest Way:** You can go to Army Tour and ask her for a boat + airport bundle which will cost you 150 baht. Tell her what time your flight is, and ask her what time you should leave. I usually recommend getting on the boat 2-3 hours before you want to be at the airport because the minivan you'll take to the airport is shared, which means it will make a few stops along the way. Book this 24 hours in advance.

○ **The Fastest Way:** Show up at Railay East pier where you'll find the longtail boat captains. They will take you to Ao Nammao Pier. There will be private drivers here who will take you directly to the airport for 400 baht. No waiting around required.

To Airport from Ao Nang

Every Tourist Kiosk offers a 150 Baht Airport Shuttle. You can book same-day!

To Surat Thani (and the East Coast Islands)

Take a 1-hour flight or take a 5-hour mini van to Surat Thani

To Koh Lanta, Koh Phi Phi and Phuket by Boat

Head to Army Tour and book a boat with them! They're your one-stop-shop, if you haven't noticed by now.

→ **To Koh Phi Phi:** 30 minutes

→ **To Koh Lanta:** 2.5 hours

→ **To Phuket:** 3.5 hours

Thai Islands

BEST FOR:

Living barefoot in your bathing suit, feeling safe as you bar hop
and beach hop.

DAYS NEEDED:

2-3 days

CHAPTER SEVEN

Thai Islands

Spending a week or two on the Thai Islands feels like being transported to another universe where your only problems are deciding whether to have two Mojitos or three.

Each island is different. While all the islands have insanely gorgeous beaches, yummy restaurants, and the ability to fit every budget - they each have their own personality.

How do you choose which one to stay on? Depends on what you're looking for, sugar!

❶ Koh Phi Phi: The Party Island

This place is super hedonistic with never ending shopping, eating, and drinking. You can walk everywhere! There are no cars here, just a maze of paved paths leading you to never-ending adventure. PLUS Koh Phi Phi is the jumping off point for some of the most stunning boat trips in Thailand. Stunning, but crowded.

❷ Koh Samui: The Easy Island

You don't have to think when you're on Koh Samui, just play and relax. This island is a big playground for travelers! That means that everything is easy. The boat trips, the walking streets, the night markets and the social life! And there's nothing wrong with easy. I love Koh Samui when I'm in the mood to mingle with other travelers on a whitesand beach, be pampered and indulge myself.

❸ Koh Phangan: The Low Key Party Island

Koh Phangan is best known for the Full Moon Party - which has branded it as a party island. But this party island has opportunities to get away from the crowds! The catch: You need to know how to drive a motorbike and drive it well over hills. If you can do that, you can unlock some stunning beaches. If you can't, you will party on some stunning beaches instead.

❹ Koh Tao: The Scuba Divers' Island

Come here to scuba dive or get your scuba dive certification, to walk along cobblestone streets eating and shopping…but no partying. This island is notorious for date rape, murders and suspicious "suicides". If you go looking for trouble, you'll find it on Koh Tao. If you snorkel, stay relatively sober, enjoy the beaches during daylight hours and are in bed by 10, I feel comfortable sending you here. I'm serious. Read the chapter.

WANT MORE ISLANDS THAN THIS?

You need my Thailand Islands and Beaches Guidebook full of the best lesser-traveled islands in Thailand.

Why a separate book? These islands are easy to weave into your big Thailand extravaganza. The other islands take more time and effort to get to and are considered off-the-beaten-path.

This book is the bucket list Thailand experience.

The Islands and Beaches book is for explorers who want to push the boundaries of traveling solo.

Get it here ☞

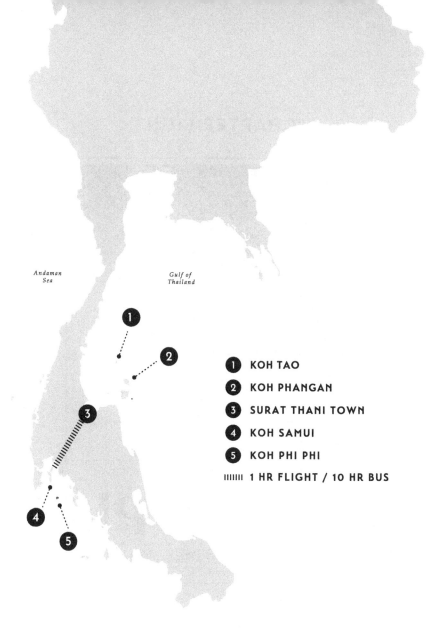

Andaman
Sea

Gulf of
Thailand

1 KOH TAO

2 KOH PHANGAN

3 SURAT THANI TOWN

4 KOH SAMUI

5 KOH PHI PHI

⦚⦚⦚⦚⦚ 1 HR FLIGHT / 10 HR BUS

♥ Koh Samui is the island with the most 'Western' amenities.

♥ Koh Tao is the famous diving island.

♥ Koh Phangan and Koh Phi Phi are big party destinations.

You get the picture.

CHAPTER EIGHT

Koh Phi Phi

———————•———————

BEST FOR:

Snorkel trips and beach parties

DAYS NEEDED:

2 minimum

———————•———————

KOH PHI PHI

CHAPTER EIGHT

Koh Phi Phi

•———————•———————•

Koh Phi Phi is known for 2 things: pristine beaches and wild parties.

You get the best of both worlds here. Spend the day snorkeling with schools of colorful fish and the nights with buckets of booze on the beach. The cobblestone streets are lined with both western and Thai restaurants alongside clothing shops, party bars, and tattoo shops.

Stay near Tonsai Pier if you're looking to be within walking distance to the social scene or nestle into one of the many private beaches if it's peace and that quiet you're looking for.

📍 ***Rough Location of Koh Phi Phi:*** Off the southwest coast of Thailand near Krabi.

↻ How to Get There: There are ferry boats that leave every day from the following locations…

- ♥ Krabi Town
- ♥ Railay Beach
- ♥ Ao Nang Beach
- ♥ Phuket
- ♥ Koh Lanta

Or you can...

 ○ Take a 2-hour Speedboat from Phuket

○ Take a 3-hour Speedboat from Krabi

HEADS UP: When you land, you'll pay a 20 baht entrance fee to the island.

Ps. Don't be discouraged when you dock on Koh Phi Phi and see a Burger King. I know I know - this is outrageous. Just keep heading inland and you'll escape this crap.

STORYTIME:

Honestly, I was afraid to come to Koh Phi Phi the last time I was in Thailand because I knew that I would be drunk within seconds of landing on the island. And so I only booked one night - so that I could update this chapter - but not even my short schedule could save me from party mode. I met a really cool girl on the boat ride over. And then, as you do on Koh Phi Phi, I walked past the bar where she was drinking with her friend. She invited me to have a drink and before I knew it, I was on a boat trip with her, her friend and a shit ton of beers. It was the drunkest, funniest, most beautiful 24 hours of my trip.

So let that be a warning to you. You will make friends on Koh Phi Phi and you will get drunk. Remember to drink water!

Island Breakdown

The Phi Phi Islands are shaped like a pair of lungs. So, for this guide, we're going to break the island down into two parts: left lung and right lung.

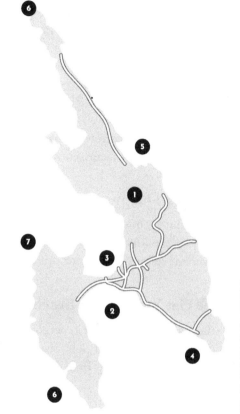

1. **THE RIGHT LUNG**
2. **TON SAI BAY**
3. **LOH DALUM**
4. **HAT YAO OR LONG BEACH**
5. **LOH BAGAO BAY**
6. **HAT LAEM THONG BEACH**
7. **MONKEY BEACH**
8. **THE LEFT LUNG**
9. **MAYA BAY**
10. **LOH SAMA BAY**
11. **PILEY BAY**

❶ The Right Lung

The right lung is the larger lung, abundant with stunning white sand beaches, rolling hills, and beautiful scenery. Over here, you'll find more than 100 resorts ranging from luxury hotels to budget accommodations – and plenty of adventure.

❷ Ton Sai Bay

The heart of the Phi Phi Islands is Tonsai Bay. Lined with cobblestone streets, everything is within walking distance – including the busiest party beach, all the best restaurants, tour shops, pharmacies and anything else you'd expect to find in a small Thai tourist town.

❸ Loh Dalum

The #1 party beach is accessible from Tonsai Bay. Here at Loh Dalum, expect a tropical exotic paradise perfect for sunbathing during the day, and wild parties with fire spinners and bucket drinks at night.

❹ Hat Yao or Long Beach

Long Beach is known for its gorgeous hikes and viewpoints above ground, and its thriving coral reefs below. There are a handful of guest houses here, perfect if you want to get away from the social scene and into nature.

❺ Loh Bagao Bay

As close as you'll get to a secret beach on Koh Phi Phi! People who complain that Koh Phi Phi is too crowded have definitely not yet discovered the virgin sands of Loh Bagao Bay. Hidden on the northeast coast of Koh Phi Phi, Loh Bagao Bay is home to The Phi Phi Island Village Resort – one of the most exclusive resorts on the island. There are no tour boats, just white sand beaches and palm trees. For even more adventure, beside the resort is a small village with mangrove forest, exciting trails, bars, and restaurants.

The easiest way to get here is from Lana Bay and Nui Beach. For serious adventurers who prefer to see beautiful hills and breathtaking sceneries, try the 2-hour hike from Loh Dalum that would take about two hours. You can always hire a local guide to help you navigate the area.

⑥ Hat Laem Thong Beach

Imagine the soothing sound of the waves or the feel of fine white sand in between your toes! A kilometer-long white sand beach awaits you at Hat Laem Thong! Also called Golden Bay, Hat Laem Thong is the ideal beach for travelers who long for a quiet and relaxing holiday. This is a secluded and serene spot perfect for zenning out.

⑦ Monkey Beach

One of the best snorkeling spots on Phi Phi can be found at Monkey Beach, aka Yong Gasem Bay. More than one hundred-meters of fine white sand fill up with curious monkeys! Just watch your bag!

⑧ The Left Lung

Uninhabited and unspoiled, the left lung is called "Phi Phi Leh". To preserve the ecosystem, no one is allowed to stay here overnight. That means no hotels and no resorts. However, you can explore the left lung with a boat trip! Phi Phi Leh is abundant with natural cliffs, caves, and canyons waiting for you to explore!

⑨ Maya Bay

The famous "secret beach" from Leonardo DiCaprio's movie "The Beach" has recently reopened after it was closed to revive the damaged coral reef. Sharks have returned and the reef is thriving but here's the catch: we can't swim here. You can take photos on the shore but if you go too far into the water, a dude with a whistle will call you out.

⑩ Loh Samah Bay

Just a few minutes from Maya Bay is a small green island called Loh Samay Bay. It's the perfect snorkeling spot teeming with marine life and colorful fish.

⑪ Piley Bay

The rock formations and the turquoise waters of Piley Bay are mesmerizing. Another fantastic spot for snorkeling, the water here is crystal clear – almost magnetizing the coral below you. Here, the fish are not scared of you, surrounding your as you swim.

Where to Stay in Koh Phi Phi

I'm going to give it to you straight. Here's the deal with Koh Phi Phi Accommodation...

Every hotel and hostel offers a slice of paradise...but on a party island. Don't expect super tranquil evenings with the sound of trickling water to lull you to sleep. Phi Phi is for boat trips during the day and cocktails at night. Once you accept these party vibes, you can truly enjoy your hotels for being a place to rest your head in-between some epic adventures! Note that the closer you are to Tonsai Pier, the bigger the party (and louder the noise).

P.P. Blue Sky Resort

Location, location, location. Eat breakfast by the beach with an undisturbed view of the waves crashing on the shore. P.P. Blue Sky Resort is the peaceful getaway that you needed. Take some 'me time' in your private bungalow or grab a snorkel and get in touch with your inner mermaid.

♥ **Style:** Privates
💸 **Budget:** $$$
📍 **Where:** Long Beach
🏨 **Address:** Longbeach, Koh Phi Phi, 138/2, Moo 7

BOOK HERE

Viking Nature Resort

If you're looking for a mixture of relaxation and party time, here's what you're going to do! Spend 2 nights at any other hotel in this section and then move over to Viking Nature Resort. This resort is not within walking distance too much on Koh Phi Phi...which means that you are going to cozy into your rustic bungalow, read a book in your hammock and just chill. This is a super unique resort to find on a party island like Koh Phi Phi, so take advantage.

- ♥ **Style:** Private Bungalows
- 💵 **Budget:** $$
- 📍 **Where:** Long Beach
- 🏨 **Address:** 222 Moo.7, Aonang, Koh Phi Phi

BOOK HERE

• •

U Rip Resort

Breakfast overlooking the ocean, anyone? Step straight off the restaurant steps into the sand at U Rip Resort. A brand-new resort in Phi Phi, U Rip offers comfortable hotel amenities to transport you into vacation mode on arrival. You've got a spacious pool with lounge beds, lush green jungle trees all around, a restaurant on site, gorgeous views of the island, and a tour desk to help you arrange a day of island hopping. Nestled into the hills and just a 10-minute walk to the center – you get the best of both worlds at U Rip.

- ♥ **Style:** Privates
- 💵 **Budget:** $$
- 📍 **Where:** Tonsai Bay
- 🏨 **Address:** 65 moo.7 T. Ao-nang

BOOK HERE

• •

PP Charlie Beach Resort

Party girls…you're going to want to check out PP Charlie Beach Resort. Nicer than a hostel but more budget-friendly than a fancy resort, here is your happy medium where you can finally meet travelers outside of the budget backpacker scene. Daily pool parties with live DJs offer the perfect opportunity to mingle with cute boys and fellow travel girls.

HEADS UP: If you're looking for peace and quiet – it's only found after the clubs die down! Sleep when you're dead, babe.

- ♥ **Style:** Privates
- 💵 **Budget:** $$
- 📍 **Where:** Central
- 🏨 **Address:** 104 Moo 7, PP Island

BOOK HERE

Blanco Beach Bar

100% guaranteed to meet people, make friends, and have a great time when you stay at this party hostel right on the beach! Join the crazy Blanco Boat Party's to Maya Bay every day and return for beach parties and events every night. Bring your bathing suit, party dresses… and maybe some ear plugs if you plan to go to bed early. This place is so much fun!

♥ **Style:** Dorms
💵 **Budget:** $
♥ **Where:** 10 Minutes from Tonsai Pier
- Loh Dalum Bay
🏬 **Address:** Loh Dalum Bay, Mu 7, Ao Nang

BOOK HERE

P2 Woodloft - *The Quiet Hotel*

I stayed at P2 Woodloft on my most recent visit to Koh Phi Phi. It's a new boutique hotel on the island and the most quiet! That is precisely why I chose this hotel: because it's hard to find a place to sleep with no light and no noise. P2 Woodloft did not disappoint, even while being centrally located! Make sure you check out their rooftop chill space!

♥ **Style:** Privates
💵 **Budget:** $$
♥ **Where:** Walking Street
🏬 **Address:** 139 Moo7

BOOK HERE

Things to Do in Koh Phi Phi

#1 Thing to Do: Take a Boat Trip

Go to Maya Bay, the Blue Lagoon and Monkey Island. You can join a group trip or you can do what I did - rent a private boat for around 3,500 baht ($100 USD), bring beers, water and snacks and then take your time going to each spot. The added benefit to getting your own boat is that you're not forced to dock at each place with 18 other tourists in your boat. The best way to do this is to find some new friends or people at your hostel to share a boat with.

Check out my Koh Phi Phi Instagram highlight to see this trip!

Ps. Maya Bay is a total Instagram vs. Reality situation. Prepare for tons of tourists hogging the beach and having shameless photoshoots. You will be able to find your own little slice of real estate and wade into the water. Emphasis on wade because you're not allowed to swim here. It's an area that is now protected. Maya Bay became so famous after the movie The Beach with Leo DiCaprio that us tourists completely assassinated the biodiversity here. Thank you to Thailand for honoring this natural wonder and protecting it. With all that being said… somehow this place is still worth the visit. It's an earthly wonder.

♥ Where: Go towards Slinky Bar where you'll see a little boat hut before the beach. Ask for Lemon. The boat captains here will hook you up.
⊙Best Time to Depart: 8am (to avoid the hottest heat) or 3pm (to avoid the tourists).

PRO TIP! Ask the captains if the weather conditions will be okay at 3pm. The afternoon waves tend to get rockier in the afternoon.

WEIRD THING: We gave Lemon a 50% deposit the day before our trip and in exchange, my friend pretended she was going to hold his bucket hat as collateral. He let her. She wore it to the bars and luckily didn't lose it before she returned it the next day. This is how trusting people are on this island. Honor the trust!

Blanco Boat Party - Island Hopping

A party boat that beach hops! If you like to get social and boozy under the sun on the open ocean, honey this is for you! Lunch is included, as are kayaks, snorkels and new friends. The drinks aren't free but they are cheap! The best deal on drinks that you'll find on a trip like this! Don't be afraid to come solo, there are plenty of solo travelers here as this is a boat cruise put on by Blanco Hostel.

On this trip you'll visit Monkey Beach, Blue Lagoon, Maya Bay, Loh Samah Bay, Viking Cave and you'll finish with sunset! Book here ☞

🏷 **Budget:** 1300 thb / $45 USD
🕑 **Open:** 1:30pm - 7pm, every Monday, Wednesday, Friday and Saturday

Snorkel with Reef Sharks

Yes, sharks! They won't bite, don't worry. On this eco-friendly snorkel trip, you snorkel with tropical fish, gorgeous corals and sharks but you'll also visit some of the most iconic spots around Koh Phi Phi including Maya Bay (where the movie "The Beach" was filmed). Because this trip is eco friendly, bring your own water bottle (not plastic) and wear eco-friendly sunscreen to keep the fish safe!

🏷 **Budget:** $30 USD/1,000 Baht   🌐 **Book Here:**

Koh Phi Phi Viewpoint

If you swipe through Tinder in Thailand, you'll come across the same scenic photo where a dude is standing on top of a mountain and below is a narrow strip of land between two beaches. That's this place. The hike offers 3 viewpoints that reach up to 186 m above sea level. The walk is only about 15–25 minutes but get ready to sweat—it's steep!

🐚 Budget: $1 USD/30 Baht (for the first 2 viewpoints) and $1.75 USD/50 Baht (for the 3rd)

Semi Private - Koh Phi Phi Island Tour

Girls, Koh Phi Phi can get super duper crowded! The beaches are small and the boat tours are full of tourists that all hit the beaches at the same times! But if you want to avoid the influencers, you can go on this tour that does their best to get you away from the crowds so you can enjoy the beaches and snorkel without tons of people around you.

🐚 Budget: $90 USD/3,000 Baht   ⊕ *Book here:*

Private Boat Tour to Swim with Plankton at Night

Okay, by now you have watched the move "The Beach" and you know what bioluminescent plankton are. Those glittering orbs that light up the water at night! This is something that everyone should experience at least once in their life. This boat trip is private, includes watching the sunset over the islands and visiting Monkey Island!

🐚 Budget: *$103 USD/3,397 Baht*   ⊕ *Book here:*

Go Scuba Diving

Go beyond coral reefs by getting your PADI certification on Koh Phi Phi. There are ship wrecks to see, manta rays to swim with and even small sharks to hang out with. The course usually lasts 2–3 days and sometimes comes with accommodation or accommodation discounts depending on where you dive.

📎 *Budget:* Open Water courses $103 USD/3,500 Baht

Ibiza Pool Party

Every day from 2pm–6pm, Ibiza throws a pool party where travelers gather to drink, swim and socialize as the live DJ spins some island-worthy tunes. This is the perfect opportunity for you solo girls to make some friends—the vibes here are always super welcoming.

📎 *Budget:* $8 USD/200 Baht admission that includes one free drink

Phi Phi Pirate Boat Booze Cruise

What would a pirate boat be without drunken sailors? While most boat tours frown upon drinking alcohol on board, the Phi Phi Pirate Boat brings the liquor for you! You'll spend the day partying AND sightseeing along with a DJ, insane views, and amazing captains to lead the adventure.

The tour stops at the most popular destinations, including Monkey Beach, Viking Cave, Pileh Lagoon, Loh Samah Bay and Sunset Point. You'll have the option of snorkeling, kayaking, or just relaxing on board with a beer. Take off is at 12:30 every afternoon with the tour ending at sunset. All you need is a swim suit and a ticket, and one of those is optional.

PRO TIP! If you've come to Phi Phi alone and want to make friends fast – this is the way to do it.

📎 *Budget:* Starts at $39/ 1300
📍 *Where:* Phi Phi Pier   ⊕ *Book here:*

Monkey Beach

Venture over to monkey beach on foot, kayak or longtail boat. Here is a pristine piece of land where you can sunbathe, snorkel, and watch a curious collection of monkeys. It's quite entertaining to watch the monkeys try to grab people's bags and drink out of coke cans- but they'll run off with your stuff if you're not careful. Ps. The water here is absolutely beautiful.

📣 **Budget:** Free

📷 @ESKARSTEIN

MONKEY FACT!

There around 5 species of monkeys in Thailand. But the ones you'll most commonly see are called "macaques". These guys are cute but they can be agressive. Monkeys in Monkey Beach are used to snatching food (and other items) from tourists, so beware!

Where to Eat in Koh Phi Phi

Everything is within walking distance on Koh Phi Phi. Just start wandering around and you'll get familiar with the cobblestone streets and establishments in no time. Use GoogleMaps and you'll find everything in a jiffy.

Garlic 1992

A family-owned restaurant that makes you feel like you're eating at your grandma's house…if your grandma was Thai and fabulous. Sit down at Garlic 1992 and you'll likely be given a little pamphlet with a mini Thai language lesson; Grandma wants to help you learn Thai. Look at the big wall with the timeline of Koh Phi Phi, it shows you how the island has changed especially before and after the tsunami destroyed the island in 2004.

Oh shit, the food. I haven't even mentioned food! It's all good, especially the Khao Soi. This is the kind of place you'll eat at once or twice a day, every day. Ps. Look for my sticker outside on the wall and take a picture for me!

Only Noodles Pad Thai

This island restaurant makes one dish and one dish only- and damn, do they make it well. Choose your style of noodles and your protein and you'll have fresh Pad Thai made to order for less than 100 baht.

Dubliners Irish Pub

Burgers, Bangers, and Banana Pancakes- when you need flavor from home, Dubliner's has got you covered. You can expect tasty western food at western prices that come in massive portions to hit the spot.

Tuk's BBQ

Head over to Reggae Bar and keep your eye out for the street vendor grilling up smokey sticks of meat and veggies starting at 30 baht each. This is true to the Thai Street Food tradition that every traveler should experience.

Effe Mediterranean Cuisine

When you want a break from Thai food, order a big ol' kebab. Kebabs are the best drunk food, if you didn't already know! Another great drunk food is their Turkish pizza! Or if you're trying to get healthy, you can order grilled chicken and vegetables which comes in a portion as big as your head.

Burger Shop

Yep, that's the name. Creative, right? I stumbled here one night leaving the fire show on the beach and was lured in by the glowing bright yellow signage like the drunk moth that I am. Burger Shop is a bar-style food stand with a million burger options to choose from. Usually I don't trust these kind of places but hey, I was drunk and hey, whatever I ordered I absolutely loved...from what I can remember.

Papaya

Eat where the locals eat...and where the tourists eat! Everyone eats at Papaya and for good reason- their Thai food and Indian dishes are incredible! Made with Muslim influence, you've got your choice of classic garlic prawns or get eastern with some freshly made naan and curry. As this place is a Muslim establishment, BYOB or order a coconut milkshake!

....oh, and McDonalds. Yep That's here now.

Nightlife in Koh Phi Phi

Kong Siam

The best live music bar on Koh Phi Phi is easily Kong Siam. The cover band puts on a fabulous, interactive show every night that creates a social atmosphere with good vibes all around. Good at singing? Kong Siam also has an open-mic every night!

Hippies Bar

Devastated in the 2011 Tsunami, Hippies Bar is back and better than ever. Take your shoes off and stick your toes in the sand while you set up shop at a driftwood table under the palm trees, overlooking the ocean. Hippies Bar streams live sports events from home and also plays live music after 8pm along with fire dancing and DJs. Cocktails are decently priced and food is fantastic.

Phi Phi Reggae Beach Bar

Muay Thai and Mojitos are the perfect combination for a rowdy night on this island paradise. Fights kick off at 9pm for an organized slice of chaos. Lots of opportunities to mingle with strangers and have a fun time

Loh Dalum Beach

Start at Slinky Bar and keep going. Wander down to the main beach lined with a collection of bars whose patrons melt together to create one big party. Some bars paint everyone with fluorescent face paint, others have bean bags on the beach positioned to watch the fire show, and most offer massive fishbowl buckets of booze to get tipsy.

PRO TIP! Skip the buckets. The booze they use might be homemade and give you a terrible hangover. Beer is a safer bet.

How to Get Around Koh Phi Phi

Walk

No cars here. Just cobblestone streets and feet!

Private Boat

Want to head to a secret beach or private bay? Or just want to do a big loop around Koh Phi Phi with some beers for your own mini booze cruise? Head to Mr. Lemon at the boat shack near Slinky Bar and see what deal you can strike up.

And that's it...on to the next island!

@BEKOZ

CHAPTER NINE

Koh Samui

- • -

BEST FOR:

Snorkel trips, beach resorts, night markets and partying

DAYS NEEDED:

3 minimum

- • -

KOH SAMUI

CHAPTER NINE

Koh Samui

●————————●

You know those blacklight mosquito traps that you turn on at night? They are so bright that they attract all of the mosquitos to one small area and leave the rest of the space totally mosquito-free. Koh Samui is kind of like that.

The blacklight lamp on Koh Samui is called Chaweng Beach.

The tourists are all here leaving the rest of the island only slightly buzzing with tourists. Have I lost you yet? What I'm trying to say is that the beauty of Koh Samui is this:

✳ Half of the island is totally developed with infinity pool resorts and live music venues – attracting the tourists and travelers.

✳ The other half of the island is unspoiled and well-preserved with waterfalls, gorgeous beaches and prime snorkeling spots.

For the solo girl who is working with a tight schedule but still wants to experience a tropical island, Koh Samui is the best bet. It's relatively easy to get to and once you're here- you can stay put while soaking up all the Thai culture, beaches, and activities you can handle. As an almost perfect circular island with a road wrapping all the way around, carefully hop on a scooter and explore.

♀ Rough Location: Off the southeast coast of Thailand in the Surat Thani Province

♺ How to Get There:

By Boat: Take a 45-minute Ferry Boat from Surat Thani Pier or one of the nearby islands.

By Plane: Fly into Koh Samui International Airport

📷 @JETSETCREATE

How dreamy is this photo?

Island Breakdown

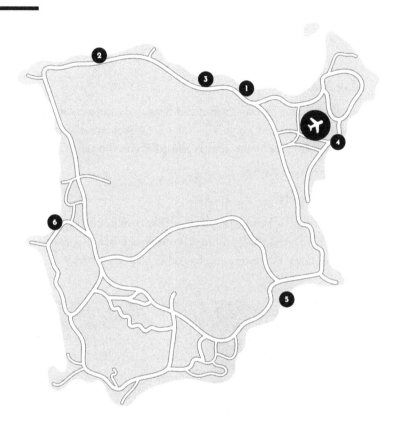

1 BOPHUT BEACH
2 MAE NAM
3 SILENT BEACH
4 CHAWENG BEACH
5 LAMAI BEACH
6 LIPA NOI BEACH

On this island, each beach has their own personality and sets the tone for the kind of vacation you'll create for yourself.

❶ Bophut Beach

Also known as Fisherman's Village, Bophut has a boutique feel to it where everything just feels personal! Stay here for a week and people will start to recognize your face. As for the beach, I call it "Body Scrub Beach," in that the sand is grainy but soft. The water is perfect for a shallow dip and a DIY scrub.

❷ Mae Nam

For the girl who came here for the beaches, head to the quiet coast of Mae Nam. The sand is powdery and white. The water is turquoise and warm. Staying in Mae Nam is perfect for luxury resorts and quiet guesthouses!

❸ Silent Beach

Also known as Ban Tai Beach, this place feels like Samui's best kept secret. Down a long jungle road is this peaceful and pristine white beach that shares its shores with the ultra-fancy W Hotel and a few other lazy beach bars.

📷 @TAYLOR.G.SIMPSON

❹ Chaweng Beach

The most western area and home to the best nightlife on Koh Samui, Chaweng Beach is a great place to set up camp. Bars, restaurants, hotels, shopping – it's all here.

❺ Lamai Beach

Lamai is the 2nd most popular vacation beach, situated just below Chaweng. The sand is soft, the water is great for swimming, and the energy is a bit toned down compared to Chaweng, while still offering options in terms of hotels and nightlife.

❻ Lipa Noi Beach

The central west coast beach, Lipa Noi offers the best sunset views! Lipa Noi has a more "beach town" feel with a collection of bars and restaurants with chilled out vibes, yet plenty of options when it comes to food and budget.

TRAVEL NOTES:

....

....

....

....

....

Where to Stay in Koh Samui

MAENAM

Khwan Beach Resort

Have you died and gone to glamping heaven? Quite possibly, yes. Khwan Beach Resort is the most surreal hotel stay you'll have this entire trip. The pool is bright and spacious with a massive waterfall and inviting swim-up bar. The glamping tents don't feel like tents…but don't feel like villas either. They have princess style beds, lavish bathtubs and even a backyard. Equipped with air-conditioning, they are comfortable in dry season. And because they're tents, they are exciting to sleep in during rainy season.

💳 **Budget:** $$$
📍 **Where:** 5-minute walk to Maenam Beach

BOOK HERE

Treehouse Silent Beach Resort

One of Mae Nam's best kept secrets, Treehouse Silent Beach Resort is pure zen. Silent Beach has white sand and clean water for swimming. The bungalows range from backpacker-budget huts to mid-range sea view villas with air-conditioning. The restaurant is my favorite on the island – known for healthy food made with clean ingredients. Try the Mojitos – they come in every flavor. The bar lights up with tiki torches at night. Have a drink here and then walk down to the swanky W Hotel and pretend to be fancy in their beachfront palace bar. *Heads Up!* Intimate and exclusive, sometimes you can only book through their website - tree-house.org

❤ **Style:** Privates
💳 **Budget:** $$
📍 **Where:** Bophut Beach
🏛 **Address:** 12/2 Moo 1 Soi Rainbow Maenam

BOOK HERE

W Koh Samui

My #1 pick for a luxury resort on Koh Samui! W Koh Samui will throw you into full-on vacation mode the second you arrive. Stay in a private pool villa where you can turn the music up and tan topless with a pool that is big enough to do laps. When you're ready to put your top back on, head to the pool.

The infinity pool here is truly an art piece, overlooking the bluest water and whitest sand you've ever seen. When you're not sunning, go for a walk on the powdery beach. This is heaven.

BONUS! They will also help you arrange your COVID test before you fly back home.

♥ **Style:** Privates
💸 **Budget:** $$$$$
📍 **Where:** Mae Nam
🛏 **Address:** 4/1 Moo1 Tambol Maenam

BOOK HERE

📷 BOOKING.COM

BOPHUT & FISHERMAN'S VILLAGE

The Waterfront Boutique Hotel

The best and most affordable resort in Fisherman's Village! The Waterfront is located at the very end of the walking street – which means no noise but instant access to all the best shopping and restaurants. It's also located at the very end of Bophut Beach – which means peace, privacy, and the cleanest water. Flop on a lounge chair in the sand and run into the sea when you get too hot.

Back in the bungalows, you've got a fabulous rain shower and one of the comfiest beds I've ever slept in. Breakfast in the morning is cooked to order and the British owner, Robin, is around to give you local tips...or just shoot the shit.

♥ **Style:** Privates
💸 **Budget:** $$$
📍 **Where:** Bo Phut Beach
🏨 **Address:** 71/2 M. 1, Bo Phut, Koh Samui

BOOK HERE

Riviera Hotel

Get the sea view room. I guarantee that you won't make it 24 hours without looking out and saying "Oh my god" at least once. This tiny 3-story guest house makes you feel like you are waking up IN the ocean. The beds are huge, there are English channels on TV and the balcony is everything!!! To get your tan on, go downstairs and drag a bean bag to the sand. Flop down and people watch until you're ready to go explore Fisherman's Village.

♥ **Style:** Privates
💸 **Budget:** $$$
📍 **Where:** Bophut Beach
🏨 **Address:** 6/1 M.1, Bophut, Fisherman's Village

BOOK HERE

CHAWENG

The Library

When a resort has a "pillow menu," you know it's going to be fancy. Famous for its bright red infinity pool overlooking the water and futuristic architecture, The Library is a splurge that's worth it just for the photos alone! Rooms range from "Smart Studios" with 42-inch plasma TVs with all the good channels to "Secret Pool Villas" that are just over the top. You must try The Drink Gallery and The Tapas Bar where they're just as creative with cocktails and dishes.

The cherry on top is that The Library is on Chaweng Beach and close to all the action including night markets and beach bars.

♥ *Style:* Privates
💸 *Budget:* $$$$
📍*Where:* Chaweng Beach
🏫 *Address:* 14/1 Moo.2 Chaweng Beach,
Bo Phut, Koh Samui

BOOK HERE

. . . .

Montien House

Instead of staying at the coveted beach club, Ark Bar, stay right next door. You can remain within walking distance to the action but get some actual sleep without techno music blaring in your dreams. Montien House is sandwiched between the best of Chaweng with the best shopping and restaurants on one end, and the beach on the other. The pool villas here are amazing and affordable – by the way! They are spacious, clean, and a fun place to bring a boy (just sayin').

♥ *Style:* Privates
💸 *Budget:* $$
📍*Where:* Chaweng Beach
🏫 *Address:* 5 Moo 2, Bophut, Koh Samui

BOOK HERE

Lub d Hostel and Beachfront Resort

Lub d Koh Samui is the newest edition to the glamourous Lub d hostel network. Feeling more like a social resort than a hostel, you'll find that everything here is just a little bit…extra. From the beachfront catamaran hammocks to the Floating DJ booth, swim up bar and infinity pool… there's no reason to stay anywhere else if tropical vibes are what you're after. Lub d Samui offers accommodation to suit all styles, from the thriftiest of backpackers to the fanciest Flashpackers (backpackers with a bigger budget)! Pack your cutest suits. Vacation starts here.

Ps. Lub d translates to "sleep well" in Thai, and here on Koh Samui - it's nodifferent. Sleep safe, sleep well, and if you're going to miss sleep, they'll give you a party worth missing sleep for.

♥ **Style:** Dorms & Privates
💸 **Budget:** $
📍 **Where:** Chaweng Beach
🏠 **Address:** 159/88 Moo 2, Bophut Koh Samui

BOOK HERE

OFF THE BEATEN PATH

Sea Valley Hotel & Spa

A picturesque resort nestled under palm trees next to the ocean away from the tourist scene on Koh Samui – Sea Valley is a must if you've got a couple days to spare. Hours melt away easily at this resort. After a fabulous breakfast, float between the pool, the beach, and the free kayaks that glide over this especially calm bay. End the day with some pampering spa services to nourish your newly sun-kissed skin.

💸 **Budget:** $$$
📍 **Where:** Lipa Noi Beach

BOOK HERE

Where to Eat in Koh Samui

If you're planning dinner, check the night market schedule first.

Night Markets...
- **Monday:** Mini Fisherman's Village Walking Street
- **Thursday:** Mae Nam Night Market
- **Friday:** Fisherman's Village Walking Street
- **Sunday:** Lamai Night Market
- **Daily:** Chaweng Night Market, Chaweng Walking Street, Lamai Night Plaza

The Black Pearl

It's always a good sign when you see both Thai and Western people eating in a restaurant! I was introduced to this secret spot by a local Thai girl. Sitting at the very end of Lamai Beach, the sand is powdery soft and the rock formations in the water make for a great view while you eat. Order the whole grilled fish (Nam Pla) and Green Papaya Sala (Som Tam)—just let them know how spicy you like it. They've got lots of fresh squid, shrimp and veggie plates, too—and for super reasonable prices.

⊙ **Open:** Daily 8am–10:30pm
♥ **Where:** Lamai
🚉 **Address:** 127/64 Moo 3, Maret

No Stress

It's impossible to be anything but totally euphoric at this beachfront bistro – hence the name. Take a break from the sun and pop in for a fresh and nutritious lunch with an ocean view. Massive burgers, seafood BBQ, and the must-try Scandinavian Mussels are enough to put you into a full-on food coma. But don't worry, they have lounge chairs on the beach perfect for a quick nap.

⊙ **Open:** Daily 8:30am – 6pm   ♥ **Where:** Lamai Beach

The Islander Pub & Restaurant

Amazing nachos. Juicy burgers. Thick steak. How does that sound? Add some classic cocktails and cheap beers and you've got it made at The Islander. Sports fans, they've got games going on big screens around the bar. If you've got a particular game coming up, let the manager know.

⊙ **Open:** Noon to Midnight   ♀ **Where:** Central Chaweng Beach

Feel Travel Samui Thai Restaurant

Authentic Thai food made for a western palate means not too spicy and nothing too crazy! Travel is a popular spot for Thai Food beginners. Start with something you know, like Pad Thai and Spring Rolls, and add in something you don't know, like Penang Curry or Pad See Ew noodles. If there was ever a time to safely step outside your food comfort zone, this is it. Ingredients are fresh, flavors are balanced, and the staff speak enough English to understand your preferences.

⊙ **Open:** Daily 6pm – 10pm   ♀ **Where:** O K Village

The Jungle Club

The views are insane here. This should be one of the first restaurants or pitstops on your trip in Samui. The Jungle Club really sets the tone for the rest of your trip. Melt into a bean bag chair and order off one of the best Thai and western tapas menus on the island. Drinks can be a bit pricey but consider it a premium for the view!

♀ **Where:** Bophut   🏠 **Address:** Soi Panyadee, Bophut, Koh Samui

Silent Beach Resort

The most popular dish on the menu is one you've got to try: Khao Soi. This northern noodle soup is served with juicy chicken in a fragrant coconut milk broth and topped with crispy wonton noodles. It's a staple in Thai culture, but a dish that isn't very well-known in the west. Now is your chance to try something you may never find at Thai restaurants back home.

Aside from Khao Soi, Silent Beach Resort is known for their healthy, yet totally yummy menu options like hummus, falafel wraps, Indian dahl and all things vegetarian. Plus, every day there is a 4–7pm Mojito Happy Hour with 99 Baht tropical mojitos of every kind!

⊙ **Open:** Lunch–10pm
📍 **Where:** Mae Nam
🗺 **Address:** 12/2 Moo 1 Soi Rainbow Maenam

Ps. This is a super local & expat spot, not too many tourists know about this place. I find that kind of fun…

The Shack

The place to go for steak and wine! The Shack imports all of their juicy cuts of meat from lamb shanks and ribs to the juiciest steaks—even compared to the steaks you've been eating back home! And since you're on vacation in Thailand, treat yourself to a true Surf and Turf with local lobster and Tiger prawns.

⊙ **Open:** Daily 5:30pm–10:30pm
📍 **Where:** Bo Phut
🗺 **Address:** 88/3 Moo 1 Fisherman's Village, Bophut

PRO TIP! When you sit down, tell your server that "The Waterfront Resort" sent you and you should get 20% off your bill.

The Hut – Thai Food

A Thai restaurant that is jam-packed every night…even in low season! That's a damn good sign. The Hut's ambiance is simple and relaxed, run by a Thai family who hurries each dish out piping hot. They specialize in traditional curries and tempura everything! Nothing fancy, just classic food with fresh ingredients.

⊙ **Open:** Daily 1pm – 10pm / In low season, open just for dinner
📍 **Where:** Fisherman's Village, across from The Waterfront Boutique
🗺 **Address:** 3/3 Moo 1 Fisherman's Village, Bophut

Things to Do in Koh Samui

Elephant Jungle Sanctuary

There are elephants on the island! In early 2019, Elephant Jungle Sanctuary became Koh Samui's first ethical retirement home and sanctuary for elephants who have spent their lives in the tourism and logging industry.

Spend the day learning about each individual elephant at the sanctuary, where they came from, and how they are living their best life. Join the elephants on walks, take a mud bath together, join them in their "elephant shower" and feed them their daily snack.

♥ **Elephant Rule of Thumb:** If an elephant park offers elephant rides, they are not a sanctuary.

💸 **Budget:** $92 USD / 2,850 baht
🕐 **Full Day Tour:** 7am – 7:30 pm
🔄 **How to Get There:** Free pickup from your hotel on Koh Samui
🌐 **Visit:** https://elephantjunglesanctuary.com/samui/

 PRO TIP! Book in advance – the sanctuary only let's a limited number of humans in per day!

Ride a Motorbike Around the Island

If – and only if - you are comfortable on a motorbike …continue reading. The roads on Koh Samui can be chaotic in Chaweng, but once you're out of that madness - the loop road around Koh Samui is pretty fun to drive. Use your GPS, and wear one headphone in your ear to listen to directions and leave one ear free to listen to traffic. GPS has mapped everything from waterfalls, restaurants, beaches and temples. The west coast of the island is much less chaotic than driving on the east coast, by the way.

Go Snorkeling
There are two ways to get your face in the water!

○ Option 1: *By Beach*
Rent a mask for the day and beach hop by motorbike. You're after the beaches with the most preserved coral and thus, the best underwater marine life.

- ♥ Coral Cove
- ♥ Taling Ngam
- ♥ Ao Phang Ka
- ♥ Tongsai Bay Resort
- ♥ Crystal Bay Resort

○ Option 2: *By Boat*
See the boat trip in the "Best Tours" section below.

Have a Bikini Day
Nikki Beach Club and Ark Bar are the two most popular beach clubs! Drink specials, lounge chairs, DJs and the ultimate place to socialize with people from all over the world!

♥ Ark Bar is on Chaweng Beach.
♥ Nikki Beach Club is on Lipa Noi.
Write to Nikki Beach Club and see if they'll do a free hotel pick-up, something that they offer in the low-seasons or on slow-days.

Big Buddha Temple
Wat Phra Yai is the most popular Buddhist Temple on Koh Samui and for good reason, starting with its impressive size. 12-meters high and covered in reflective gold paint, Wat Phra Yai shimmers under the sun which you can see from the bottom of the 45-step staircase leading up to the giant statue. Sitting in the classic mediation pose known as "Buddha defying Mara" – or resisting temptation to reach enlightenment.

Before you head up the stairs, visit the monk sitting to the left under the shade. You can give a donation of 20 baht, and then kneel with your hands in prayer and head down, as he blesses you with incense and holy water.

Head up the stairs- just take your shoes off first- and walk around the temple as you ring each prayer bell for good luck. Want to make your dreams come true? Before you go, take a 10-baht coin, make a wish and throw it up onto Buddha's lap. If the coin stays, your wish will come true.

⦿ Where: Bophut

Visit Wat Plai Laem

In my opinion, this is the most impressive temple grounds on Koh Samui, but half as many tourists visit here! What makes this temple so special is that it combines Buddhism and Hinduism. There are countless statutes and temples that pay tribute to the gods, spirits, and ancestors – you can easily spend 30 minutes walking around in awe.

But the most awe-inspiring of all is Wat Plai Laem, the 18-arm statue of Guanyin, the Goddess of Mercy and Compassion. Colorful, unique, and #FemaleEmpowerment, Guanyin is believed to be a source of unconditional love, a protector of all beings and a fertility goddess. She is the Goddess to whom local women come to pray for a child, and healthy family.

🖾 @WILSONWANDERING

Before you go, walk towards the small shop in the center of the compound and you'll see a fish food machine. Drop in a coin, take a basket and collect your fish food that looks more like cat food. Go to the lake and start feeding the fish – you'll be shocked by all the creatures that rise up from the depths.

LOCAL TIP! Go to the fresh market next to Thong Sala Pier and buy a live turtle for about 150 baht. The lady will bag it…just make sure he can breathe! When you get to the temple, you'll cross a small bridge leading to Wat Plai Laem Temple. In this pond, you release your turtle and the god brings you good karma and luck for your deed.

♥ *Where:* Bo Phut – 1.9 miles east of Wat Phra Yai

Watch a Muay Thai Fight
When you're walking down the streets of Chaweng, you'll see and hear trucks driving through the center blasting advertising for 'big Muay Thai fight tonight!' There's always a fight going on at Chaweng Boxing Stadium, often featuring western fighters which is a pretty thrilling sight to see. **PRO TIP!** Free Muay Thai Match in Lamai on Saturday Nights from evening to 10pm. You're expected to buy a drink when you're in there – but they won't force you if you say, "Later later".

✍ *Budget:* Around 1500 baht
♥ *Where:* Chaweng Boxing Stadium

Want to try your hands at a Muay Thai Boxing Class? Try Jackie Muay Thai – 1st lesson is 400 baht

Grandma and Grandpa Rock
Can you spot Grandma and Grandpa? In Lamai, there is a gorgeous rocky peninsula that juts into the water giving you gorgeous views of Lamai beach and the bay. There's more to do here than just enjoy the view, however. There are two rocks that represent Grandma and Grandpa. Grandpa is pretty easy to find, Grandma take a bit of effort, don't be afraid to ask someone where to find her. Once you see them, congratulations, you officially understand Thai humor in a nutshell. Oh, and there are some cute boutiques and a little street market on the way down to the rocks!

♥ *Where:* Lamai

Best Tours on Koh Samui

Island-Hopping + Snorkeling + Pig Island

Spend the day on a big pirate ship boat with lounge areas where you can tan under the sun while cruising the open water. You'll stop at stunning corals to snorkel and to Koh Madsum aka Pig Island! Like the Bahamas, there are free-range pigs just running around and swimming in the ocean. If you go on any boat trip while in Koh Samui, let this be it.

Book here ☞

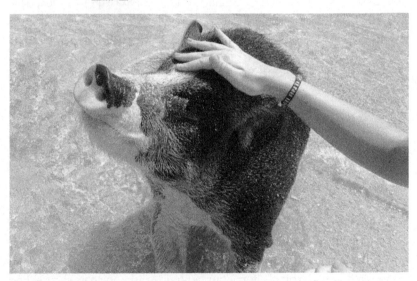

📷 GET YOUR GUIDE

Ang Thong Marine Park Day Tour

Ang Thong Marine Park is one of the most stunning underwater habitats in the Gulf of Thailand. There are 42 islands total, all with preserved corals and protected marine life. And you can see them up close with this incredible tour.

Wake up bright and early - a car will be at your hotel waiting to pick you up at 7:30 am. Next stop, the pier! You'll board a speed boat with about 30 other tourists from all over the world. You'll put on life jackets and be given a quick brief on the day. Then you'll be handed your snorkel and the fun begins.

- ♥ Island Viewpoints to see the whole Marine Park
- ♥ Small deserted white sand beaches and islands
- ♥ Snorkeling with colorful schools of fish, eels, and urchins
- ♥ Local Thai food lunch and cold bottles of water.

The whole day is a whirlwind of tropical paradise! However...this is the #1 attraction in the area which means more tourists. I only only only recommend doing it on the semi-private tour boat below where you can enjoy the view - as compared to the group tour below.

Check out these options:

Semi Private Tour ☞   Group Tour ☞

Samui Quad Bike Tour

Take your pick between a 1 or 2-hour quad bike tour through the jungles of Koh Samui. As you follow your guide over red dirt roads and small river streams, you'll pass stunning viewpoints of the ocean and island shore below. When you take the two-hour tour, you drive out to a remote waterfall in the jungle and go for a swim in the cool, clear pool below, followed by a drink at this secluded bar in the jungle.

🏷 **Budget:** $54 USD / 1800 baht
🕐 **How Long:** 1 hour
🌐 **Contact:** SamuiQuadATV.com

FUN THAI FACT! There are over 35,000 Buddhist Temples in Thailand.

Nightlife in Koh Samui

Ark Bar

Sitting on 150 meters of beach front property, Ark Bar has made the loud and clear statement that they are party central on Chaweng Beach! During the day, join the pool party with a swim up bar. At night, party goers are lured in with live DJs and fire spinners. The vibes here stay pretty mellow with tropical cocktails and beachfront lounge chairs—but the fun doesn't stop until at least 2am.

♥ Where: Chaweng Beach
◉ Open: Daily 7am–2am

ARK BAR

Hush Bar Samui

In the mood to dance and mingle? Throw yourself onto the dance floor at Hush Bar—where every night there is a different DJ spinning everything from Hip Hop & RnB to UK Garage, Commercial House, Dubstep and Drum n Bass. They've got super cheap buckets until 9pm, just remember to watch your drink and take it easy! Hush Bar's reputation is just fine—just keep your wits about you, my love. Heads Up: After Hush Bar, the crowd usually flows to the next dance/ clubbing spot—Stadium which is open til 7am.

♥ Where: Soi Green Mango, Chaweng Beach
☉ Open: Daily 7pm–2:30am

Chaweng Center

Bar hopping is the thing to do in Chaweng. Like a school of fish, people seem to flow together or follow the live music. There are hole in the wall bars, music

The most popular bars to visit on any given night:
- ♥ The Palm
- ♥ Green Mango
- ♥ Hendrix
- ♥ Stadium
- ♥ Henry Afrika

On Street Bar

Not the house-music clubbing type of gal? No problem. On Street Bar is a quirky little watering hole next to KC Beach Club—so tiny that you might miss it if you're not paying attention. Built with upcycled tin walls and decorated with a collection of colorful light fixtures and random figurines—consider this the speak easy of Koh Samui. Live music, cheap beer, good people.

♥ Where: Chaweng Rd next to KC Beach Club
☉ Open: Daily 7pm–2am

Starz Cabaret

No matter how hard us girls try, we will never be as feminine or glamourous as a lady boy—and this show proves it. At a glance, you'd never know these glamourous stage performers covered in feathers and pearls were born as boys. They are so sensual and feminine as they glide across the stage, performing choreographed dance numbers and over-the-top lip-syncing Britney Spears bits. Each show is 45 minutes long and your entrance includes one drink.

💸 **Budget:** $7 USD/220 Baht
🕐 **When:** 3 shows daily, 8:30pm, 9:30pm & 10:30pm
📍 **Where:** Chaweng, 1st floor at Khun Chaweng Resort
🏛 **Address:** 200/11 Moo 2, Chaweng Beach Rd

Coco Tam's

A must-visit, no matter where you're staying on the island. Get you cute butt up to Coco Tam's for cocktails on the beach. This sprawling beachfront bar feels like an adult playground: There are bar-side swings for chairs, catamaran style net beds, bean bags in the sand, movies every night, two pool tables, and a beer pong table. YET, they keep things real classy and vibes stay super chill. Try a margarita or a Mango Mojito. You can trust that the alcohol is western quality—so go for it, babe.

🕐 **Open:** 1pm–1am
📍 **Where:** Bophut Fisherman's Village
🏛 **Address:** 62/1 Moo 1 Bophut

Ps. Sitting on those swings all night is an easy way to get chatting to some new people!

How to Get Around Koh Samui

Grab Taxi

The Uber of Thailand. Grab Taxi is convenient because you can hook it up to your ATM card. If you run out of cash or don't want to keep track of your cash, you've got a guaranteed way to get home.

Navigo

Just like Grab Taxi and Uber, Navigo is Koh Samui's on-call driving service. I often find Navigo to be cheaper than Grab Taxi, but sometimes Grab Taxi is more convenient. It's nice to have options.

Motorbike

You can rent a motorbike on Koh Samui...but I only recommend riding during the day and avoiding driving through the busy streets of Chaweng. There is a street that loops around the whole island – it gets pretty calm on the west coast.

FUN THAI FACT!

Thailand is the sole country in Southeast Asia that was never colonised by any European nation.

CHAPTER TEN

Koh Phangan

————————•————————

BEST FOR:

Beach Parties

DAYS NEEDED:

2-3 days

————————•————————

CHAPTER TEN

Koh Phangan

———— • · · · · • ————

NOTE: *If you're coming to party, you could stay for a week and have a great time socializing and bar hopping. If you're a mild partier, 3 days on Koh Phangan is more than enough to see all there is to see! Not a partier at all? Come for 2 nights, stay at a great beach resort and then keep it moving.*

Pronounced "Ko Pan-Yang"—Koh Phangan is synonymous with parties! There's the Full Moon Party, Jungle Party, Waterfall Party and random parties every damn day of the week. While partying is certainly the main attraction on this small tropical island…there is more to Koh Phangan than just partying!

Being the fifth largest island in Thailand, Koh Phangan offers plenty of relaxing beaches and natural wonders to explore. There are day waterfalls, sand bars, viewpoints and…parties. Okay, it's a party island.

If you're coming to party, you could stay for a week and have a great time socializing and bar hopping. If you're a mild partier, 3 days on Koh Phangan is more than enough to see all there is to see!

📍 ***Rough Location:*** North of Koh Samui & South of Koh Tao, off the east coast of Thailand.

↻ *How to Get There:*

By Boat

→ Take a ~3 hour boat from Surat Thani Pier

→ Take a 30-minute boat from Koh Samui

→ Take a 1 hours speedboat from Koh Tao

These ferries leave at all times of the day with over 5 companies. Or take a Speed Boat or Ferry from Koh Samui or Koh Tao leaving multiple times per day.

♥ Half of the island is totally developed with infinity pool resorts and live music venues – attracting the tourists and travelers.

♥ The other half of the island is unspoiled and well-preserved with waterfalls, gorgeous beaches and prime snorkeling spots.

While Koh Phangan is a relatively small island, you've still got your choice of beaches.

SOLO GIRL TRAVEL TIP

On Koh Phangan, backpackers tend to rent motorbikes without knowing how to drive them…and they crash…often into other motorbikes. Always wear a helmet and pay attention to the doofus driving beside you AND be on the lookout for street dogs lying in the road.

Island Breakdown

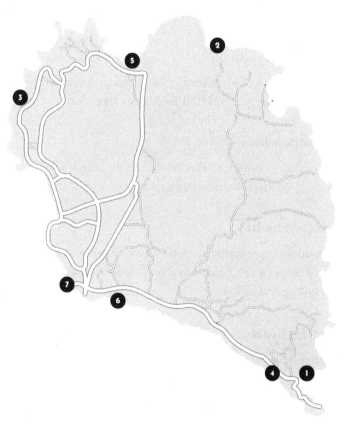

1 HAAD RIN
2 BOTTLE BEACH
3 HAAD YAO BEACH
4 LEELA BEACH
5 CHALOKLUM BAY
6 BAN TAI BEACH
7 THONGSALA PIER

① Haad Rin

is where the full moon, half moon, and other wild parties go down. This is Koh Phangan's busiest beach and beach neighborhood—always alive with energy.

② Bottle Beach

is one of my Top 10 Beaches in Thailand. Bottle Beach is stunning, unspoiled and a must-visit when on Koh Phangan. Tiny and pristine, there are only a few bungalows and restaurants tucked into the jungle, overlooking the beach.

③ Haad Yao Beach

is a gorgeous stretch of white sand within walking distance to restaurants, bars, and guest houses, staying at Haad Yao is a fabulous idea.

④ Leela Beach

is situated opposite of Haad Rin Beach with the bluest waters and the softest white sand. A few resorts are available here with every budget in mind.

⑤ Chaloklum Bay

is a tranquil beach perfect for travelers looking for complete relaxation. Activities you can engage in at Chaloklum Bay include windsurfing, kiting, surfing, wakeboarding, and diving.

⑥ Ban Tai Beach

where the party never ends. Once the sun starts to set, Ban Tai transforms into party heaven. Restaurants and bars come alive with live music, drink specials and bucket drinks. Still around, it only gets wilder.

⑦ Thongsala Pier

is my favorite area to stay in Koh Phangan, with coffee shops, craft beer, night markets and peaceful accommodation—all within walking distance to Thongsala Ferry Pier.

Where to Stay in Koh Phangan

Sarikantang Resort and Spa

On one hand, you're classy and like to spend the day sunbathing with a mojito by your side and a flower in your hair. On the other hand, you want to go to the Full Moon Party and dance your face off until the sun comes up. I feel you, girl. Sarikantang is the place to be both sophisticated and spastic. You've got this superb beachfront resort isolated on the white sands of Seekantang Beach – sunset and privacy included – which is only a 10-minute walk or free hotel tuk tuk ride to Haad Rin Center where all the partying goes down. Go have a wild night and walk home to your sanctuary when you're ready.

★ *Style:* Privates

💸 *Budget:* $$$

📍 *Where:* Seekantang Beach, 10-minute walk to Haad Rin

BOOK HERE

Wonderland Yoga Retreat

An all-inclusive yoga/detox/meditation retreat at a paradise resort in Thailand! Come, stay for 3 days. That's all you need to balance your mind, body and spirit. Or stay longer; join a yoga retreat or get your yoga or reiki certification. Wonderland has all things spiritual, healthy and relaxing including a pool under the palm trees and a full schedule of meditation and mindfulness classes. Yes, the menu is vegetarian but it's so good that you won't miss meat. And it's all included when you stay here. It's like adding a little Bali to your Thailand experience.

★ *Style:* Private Rooms + Dorms

💸 *Budget:* $$$

📍 *Where:* Tucked into the jungle - but you don't need to leave here for the entire time you're here. Slow it down, sister

BOOK HERE

Angkana Hotel Bungalows

Recharge your spiritual battery under the palm trees at Angkana's private beach resort. With only a handful of bungalows on this beachfront property, you can expect total peace and quiet. The entire resort is white sand, from reception to the shore – the sand is constantly being combed by the staff, creating this dreamlike world.

Wade out into the still waters of the shallow bay and just sit in silence. Watch the occasional fisherman putter in with his day's catch and watch the sky change from bright blue to red and then orange. Head back to your bungalow and sway the night away in your private hammock. Walk 15-minutes to Thong Sala Night Market or Thong Sala Town – an area with some of the best cafes and bistros on the island.

★ *Style:* Beach Bungalows

💵 *Budget:* $$

📍 *Where:* Thong Sala

BOOK HERE

Bamboo Bungalow Baan Tai Phangan

Like to be social but also like to have your space? Bamboo Bungalow Baan Tai Phangan is the perfect place to mingle and then retreat to your private hut. The real star of the show here is the owner who is a host, a magician and the best concierge in town. Anything you need, he will help you sort it out. There's mini golf here which is just a fun way to bring travelers together. And babe, you're not going to find a cheaper private room than this!

★ *Style:* Private Huts

💵 *Budget:* $

📍 *Where:* Baan Tai Beach

BOOK HERE

Mangata Boutique Bungalows

Heaven on earth is Mangata Boutique Bungalows. Get away from the hustle and bustle of the real world with a relaxing stay in this Instagram-worthy hotel that is just begging to be photographed! Each bungalow has its own porch surrounded by sky-high palm trees and just steps to the beach. Get a beachfront bungalow where you can watch the sunset from your private hammock.

★ *Style:* Private Bungalows

💸 *Budget:* $$$

📍 *Where:* Chao Phao Beach

BOOK HERE

• •

SeaEsta Beach

The vibes here are good and so are the drink specials! Plan to be barefoot and buzzed 90% of the time you're staying here. You'll like that the pool is big enough to swim around but small enough that chatting with your pool neighbors is inevitable. Not to mention, this is the absolute best value you're going to find for a beachfront property!

★ *Style:* Privates

💸 *Budget:* $$

📍 *Where:* Ban Tai Beach

BOOK HERE

• •

Le Divine Comedie Beach Resort

If Tulum and Thailand had a baby, this would be it. The crowd here is cool. There are digital nomads, DJs, fashionistas...but all kinda on a budget and way less pretentious than the fancy resorts. Beachfront, social vibes, amazing views, and great food - come here to get cute and mingle. You are absolutely going to make some cool friends here.

★ *Style:* Private Rooms

💸 *Budget:* $$

📍 *Where:* Baan Tai Beach

BOOK HERE

Phangan Arena Hostel

Imagine an adult summer camp! That's what Phangan Arena Hostel is. There's a soccer (footy) field, massive pool with bean bags all around for tanning, beer pong table, internet café, free gym, movie room, and non-stop bucket drinks- it's hard to pass this place up…especially for 100-baht dorm beds. The crowd is usually a mix of travelers in their 20's, very social, and carry on socializing well into the night. If you want to make a few friends, then get your cute butt over here.

♥ *Style:* Dorms and Privates

💵 *Budget:* $

📍 *Where:* Ban Tai

BOOK HERE

Where to Eat in Koh Phangan

You are most likely going to eat wherever is close to where you're staying - because remember, Koh Phangan is mountainous and not that easy to hop from village to village. So - explore!

But here are a couple of my favorite places in case you find yourself nearby!

Soho

Draft beer and craft beer—oh, how I've missed you. For beer snobs, drinking Chang all week can get pretty old. At Soho, they feature local microbrews from the region—particularly from Cambodia. They've got all your favorites on tap, too, like Carlberg and Tiger. If you're into sports, they've always got a match of some sort on the TVs and incredible Mexican food and western tapas to go along with the mood.

⊙ **Open:** 9:30am–1pm
♀ **Where:** Thong Sala
🚏 **Address:** 44/56 Moo1 Thong Sala

Café 2401 and Guesthouse

As if fabulous food weren't enough, this café sits atop a cliff overlooking the sea with views of Koh Samui in the distance. Order the most delicious bowl of Tom Yum Soup or go western with a Full English Breakfast. The ingredients are fresh, and food is made to order. Not to mention, the staff are delightful! Go go go!

⊙ **Open:** Daily 10am–3pm & 6pm–10pm
♀ **Where:** Ban Thai
🚏 **Address:** 32/4 Moo 4

Amsterdam Bar & Restaurant

Over and over on the island, I heard "we're going to Amsterdam Bar" so I had to see what the fuss was about. So, imagine a beach club that isn't actually on the beach, but rather, in the jungle with insane views of the water and beach below. That's Amsterdam Bar. It's a viewpoint bar full of travelers lounging on mats on the floor with small tables and big portions of western food. There's a pool that no one really gets in, but it sets the mood—along with the live DJ. If you're looking to mingle, this is the place to do it. Be here for sunset, it's stunning from up here.

⊙ *Open:* Daily 12pm–1am
♥ *Where:* Koh Pha Ngan
🚕 *Address:* Wok Tum, Koh Pha Ngan

House People

Under a large, farm-style thatched roof with warm, dim lighting and plenty of space between tables, this is the place to come with that cute boy you met on the ferry. Ambiance is key, and the food certainly helps. Happy hour has some great drink specials to go along with your authentic Thai food cooked with just the amount of spice that you prefer.

⊙ *Open:* Sun–Fri 3:30pm–11pm
♥ *Where:* Had Yao/Secret Beach
🚕 *Address:* Haad Yao, Ko Pha Ngan

Rasta Baby

A sub sect of Thai culture seems to overlap with old school Jamaican culture. You'll find sprinkles of places like Rasta Baby with Bob Marley music, eclectic bartenders, beers with mellow prices, and Thai food that was made with lots of love for flavor. So, when you climb the stairs to reach Rasta Baby, plan on staying for a while.

⊙ *Open:* Daily 10am–2am
♥ *Where:* Near Haad Rin
🚕 *Address:* Thong Nai Pan Noi Beach

Things to Do in Koh Phangan

Mingalaba Island Tour

You'll drive almost the entire perimeter of the island in one day, stopping off at the best beaches, climbing up one of the most gorgeous waterfalls, and exploring a natural sand bar where you can snorkel! The last stop is Three Sixty Bar for instance views of the island and a drink. On the way back, the driver will keep his eye out for monkeys and stop if he's sees them. Hop out for a quick photoshoot.

All of this is done in an intimate group of 7 or 8 people in the back of a songthaew, making it easy to make some friends.

🏷️ **Budget:** $15 USD/500 Baht
🕐 **When:** 10am–3pm (roughly)
📍 **Where:** Hotel Pickup

RESPONSIBLE TRAVELER TIP!

When you make your booking, emphasize that you DO NOT want to stop at the Elephant Riding Camp – and make the company confirm your demand. Visiting the camp is "optional" in the tour, so if people in your car ask to go there, the driver might oblige in order to receive a hefty commission from the camp. **The only way to end Elephant Riding practices is to refuse to participate.**

Slip N Fly

The best daytime party on the island, Slip N Fly proved that you're never too old to enjoy a waterslide…especially when it's 131 feet long. There's a massive pool with floaties and tanning spaces, plus drinks and a bar and boys and fun. Slip N Fly offers daily passes and Full Moon Party promotions so check out their website when you get to the island!

🏷 **Budget:** $20 USD/650 Baht
📍 **Where:** The middle of the island!
🏛 **Address:** 98/5 Moo 3 Madeuwan

Explore the National Marine Park

Over 40 tropical islands await you at Ang Thong National Marine Park.

If you missed the opportunity to explore while you were on Koh Samui, it's no problem. Jump aboard Phangan Boat Trips which will pick you up from your hotel and whisk you away for a day of hidden lagoons, coral gardens, and white sand beaches.

Book with Phangan Boat Trips here ☞

Go Snorkeling

○ *Option 1*: Rent a Mask

Rent a mask for the day and beach hop by motorbike. You're after the beaches with the most preserved coral and thus, the best underwater marine life.

◇ Mae Haad

◇ Chao Phao

◇ Haad Khom

◇ Koh Ma

○ *Option 2*: By Boat

Go into any tour office and ask about a snorkel boat trip! Just like Samui, you can join a bigger island-hopping tour like the Angthong Marine Park Day Tour that includes snorkeling but isn't all about snorkeling. Or pop into a dive center—their trips will be smaller and come with cute boys.

Thong Sala Night Market – Koh Phangan

Thanon khon dern. Road person walk. That is exactly what you do as Thong Sala Night Market comes to life in the evenings, particularly on Saturdays.

The long and narrow road is packed with food stalls selling everything from Thai donuts to quail eggs. And in proper Thai fashion, you'll find every kind of meat on a stick, as well. In the center of this walking street, there will be vendors on the ground who have laid out second hand t-shirt and toys, as well as, vendors selling leather purses, sparkly fanny packs and jewelry galore.

○ **Open:** 4pm–11pm
♥ **Where:** Thong Sala

Best Hikes on Koh Phangan

○ **Bottle Beach Hike:** 45 to 50 minutes each way

○ **Koh Ra Hike:** Expect a 20 baht entrance fee which will include a bottle of water

○ **Haad Rin to Haad Yuan:** Take the nature trail from Palita's Lodge in Haad Rin; a gorgeous beach awaits you.

PRO TIP! Use AllTrails.com to find the trail maps

Best Sunset Spots on Koh Phangan:

* Bluerama
* Top Rock
* Freeway
* Two Rocks
* Amsterdam Bar
* Three Sixty Bar
* Secret Mountain

TIP FOR SECRET MOUNTAIN BAR:

Just know, this place is on the top of an extremely steep hill, directly behind the town of Baan Tai. Only attempt this DIY mission if you're an experience scooter driver. You can look up "Secret Mountain" on Google Maps. And hey, there are usually tuk tuks waiting on the top to take you back into town after your hike.

Nightlife in Koh Phangan

Infinity Beach Club

At any and every moment, you can walk outside your front door and find a party raging on Koh Phangan. Prime example: Infinity Beach Club. With 3 bars, 2 restaurants, and 1 big ass pool occupying 1,000sqm of prime beach front property—this place is alive at all hours of the day. Bring your suit and get ready to mingle. Happy hour is between 5–6pm for discounts on food and drink.

- ⊙ *Open:* 10am—2am
- ♥ *Where:* On Baan Tai Beach, 1 mile south east of Baan Tai Pier

Fubar

Traveling solo, right? Stop by Fubar any time of day or night and make some friends. The booze is always flowing, tunes are always going, and the bartenders are always up for a decent convo. They throw live DJ parties, partake in green activities and there's always a crowd ready to go bar hopping. You don't have to be a guest to join in on the fun.

- ⊙ *Open:* 24/7… yep
- ♥ *Where:* Right on Haad Rin Beach East

Ku Club

A legit nightclub on Koh Phangan, where you come to dance your face off past midnight. It's always packed thanks to seriously talented DJs, drink specials, and an inviting open-air venue.

- ⊙ *Open:* Daily 6pm–1am
- ♥ *Where:* Baan Tai Beach
- 🏢 *Address:* The Beach Village

Koh Phangan Party Guide

📷 JOE STUMP

Full Moon Party

The famous Full Moon Party kicks off once or twice a month on Haad Rin Beach. It's such an epic party that backpackers and vacationers alike plan their entire Thailand vacation around this event. Expect tons of booze, dress in fluorescent colors, and I dare you to try and make it out of there without someone painting your face.

SOLO GIRL TIPS FOR THE FULL MOON PARTY:

🦩 Book a hotel in Haad Rin so that you can easily get back to your hotel without relying on other people or transportation.

🦩 Know that MANY hotels will require a minimum booking of anywhere from 2–5 days during the week of the Full Moon party.

🦩 Expect hotel prices to be more expensive during the Full Moon party—it's annoying but consider it an investment in fun memories!

🦩 Partygoers like to pop some fun pills here and smoke all sorts of weird stuff. Before you partake, make sure you are with a group of people who you trust and will stick with the rest of the night.

🦩 Bring an over-the-shoulder purse and don't take it off. It's so easy to lose your bag at the Full Moon Party with all the chaos—so keep your belongings close.

🦩 Watch your pockets as pick pockets prey on drunk people who have their guard down.

🦩 Drink lots and lots of water. Write the word 'water' on your hand before you go out—especially if you plan to party hard. Water will keep you from blacking out and will keep you hydrated and healthy.

Waterfall Party

Starting back in 2010, Waterfall Party has been rocking SE Asia with its massive electronic beats, gorgeous mountain views, and waterfall surroundings.

This event takes place twice a month (two days before the Full Moon Party, and two days after). Held deep in the tropical jungle of Koh Phangan, Waterfall Party has grown so popular that it now attracts recognizable international DJ's, fire shows, and acrobatic performances. Picture neon jungle, trippy glow-lights, an intense sound system, and dance party vibes! In short, if you love EDM, you want to go to this party!

And to feed all the jungle guests, there are food stalls, drink stands, market-style booths to buy jewellery and accessories for the party, and you can have yourself styled up by a professional body paint artist on site.

The party starts at 8pm and goes on for more than 12 hours. That being said, people do partake in psychedelics here...which I urge you not to do.

How do you buy tickets? You can purchase your ticket at the "door", or you can pre-book by visiting them on Facebook at Waterfall Party Koh Phangan

How do you get there? Jump in a songthaew. Most hotels organize collective transport for their guests.

How much is it? 600 Baht

SOLO GIRL TIPS FOR THE WATERFALL PARTY

🦩 If you don't feel like doing the five minute walk from the entrance of the jungle to the party area, there's a free lift service that'll take you there.

🦩 There are no ATM's on-site, so bring cash.

🦩 Things may get messy with paint and jungle, so don't wear your most expensive outfit or brand-new shoes!

🦩 It's 10 Baht to use the bathroom here.

Jungle Party

Another massive event blaring deep house, tech house, progressive and techno music, Jungle Party is set in the middle of the Baan Tai Jungle. The feeling of this party is that of shared love for dance music, togetherness, and preserving nature! You know, hippie shit.

But this event is not only a massive dance party surrounded by awesome nature— it's also a circus-like event with live art installations, tons of glitter and sparkles, colourfully painted bodies, amazing costumes, and lots of smiling faces. If you want to get "circus-y" too, there will be professional costume and body painting assistants, along with hair artists to make you look the part. For entertainment, expect Thai boxers showcasing their talent, extensive lights and lasers, and hula hoop fire dancers! It's wild.

The event takes place once a month, one day before the Full Moon Party, so if this sounds like your cup of tea, you best plan your Thailand adventure accordingly.

How do you buy tickets? You can grab a ticket at several backpacker hostels in Hat Rin and Ban Tai, or you can simply buy your ticket at the "door".

How do you get there? Jungle Party can be found in the Baan Tai Jungle in Ko Phangan. Like Waterfall Party and Full Moon Party, most party hostels will be organizing collective transportation where guests migrate together.

How much is it? 600 Baht

SOLO GIRL TIPS FOR THE JUNGLE PARTY

🦩 Only bring what you're willing to lose. Make sure you leave your ATM cards at home.

🦩 There is a first aid tent with qualified staff, free of charge.

🦩 CCTV is available throughout the area.

🦩 There are quiet zones and sleeping areas for those who want to chill

🦩 Food and drinks stalls are available so bring some cash.

SAFE GIRL TIP

If you're coming to Koh Phangan to party, it's a good idea to stay at a more social hostel that attracts other traveling party animals so you can travel to the party together. It's the safest and most fun way to participate!

Getting Around Koh Phangan

Not a Motorbike

I strongly do not recommend riding a motorbike on Koh Phangan. The roads are incredibly steep, windy and narrow with sandy patches that people wipe out on all the time.

Pair that with traffic and a collection of overconfident and sometimes, drunk travelers driving motorbikes and you've got tons of accidents.

Walk

If you're staying in the Haad Rin Area, everything you need is within walking distance! In fact, most beaches have a handful of restaurants and mom & pop shops within walking distance.

Songtheaw

Flag a Songtheaw down on the side of the road or have your hotel call one for you. On Koh Phangan, you're going to pay anywhere from 100–300 Baht for a one-way ride.

"One's destination is never a place,
but a new way of seeing things"
HENRY MILLER

Koh Tao

BEST FOR:

Getting scuba certified

DAYS NEEDED:

4-5 if you're doing an open-water dive course / 3 days if you're
just coming for a quick taste of island life

KOH TAO

CHAPTER ELEVEN

Koh Tao

•————•————•

The diving island! Koh Tao is famous for having incredible diving sites, world-renowned diving instructors, and is the most affordable place to become certified scuba diver with an Open Water Diving Course. This little island is a diver's paradise with over 50 diving schools. And as a close neighbor to Koh Phangan and Koh Samui, it's easy to add Koh Tao into your diving schedule.

When you're not diving, melt into the sand with a mojito in your hand while you watch unobstructed sunsets like you've never seen before. Beach bars are aplenty, as well as hotels and resorts. Dive hard, relax harder.

*But, party safely. Please read the Nightlife section before you come.

📍 **Rough Location:** North of Koh Phangan, off the east coast of Thailand.

↻ **How to Get There:**

→ **By Boat:** Take an 8-hour overnight boat from Surat Thani Pier, a speed boat from Koh Phangan, or a ferry from Koh Samui.

Island Breakdown

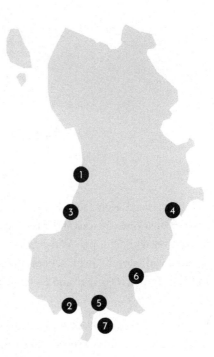

1. **SAIREE BEACH**
2. **CHALOK BAN KHAO**
3. **MAE HAAD BEACH**
4. **TANOTE BAY**
5. **HAAD THIEN**
6. **AO LEUK**
7. **SHARK BAY**

The smallest of the 3 islands, Koh Tao has a lot of diversity to offer in terms of beaches…

1 Sairee Beach

The main beach on the island! Sairee Beach is a mile-long strip of fine sand and a great spot for having cocktails while watching the sunset. Most nightlife occurs here but…again, be careful. Sairee Beach has a sinister history that most tourists know nothing about. In the daytime, Sairee Beach is welcoming and safe; but at night, there have been a few rare but serious crimes (See Koh Tao Nightlife).

❷ Chalok Ban Khao

Enjoy some modern amenities without the crowd at Chalok Ban Khao Beach. Here you'll find several dive shops, a pharmacy and a 7-Eleven store. Not to mention, the beach is gorgeous.

❸ Mae Haad Beach

Considered the capital of Koh Tao, everything you need is right here. Countless shops, restaurants, and bars are located at Mae Haad Beach. There are even ATMS and money exchanges.

❹ Tanote Bay

Adrenaline junkies will find this beach alluring, albeit a little challenging to get to. Down a bumpy dirt road, only the dedicated adventurers make their way here. Tanote Bay is one of the best snorkeling spots with bright and beautiful corals, and this is also a spot for cliff jumping. *Just get travel insurance first, please!

❺ Haad Thien

Haad Thien is one of the best beaches on Koh Tao. It's lined with coconut palm trees and water is crystal-clear. And the best part? It's not crowded at all because it's quite far from town. Stay at Haad Tien Beach Resort and you can wake up in paradise every morning.

❻ Ao Leuk

Take a break from partying and head to this quiet beach with astonishing coral reefs. Travelers who love to snorkel prefer Ao Leuk.

❼ Shark Bay

This private bay can only be accessed either by kayak or boat – and is totally worth the trip. The bay is gorgeous with fine white sand and clear water that offers amazing snorkeling with blacktip reef sharks. The best time to see the sharks is between 7 am and 10 am. You may spot some green turtles here too!

Where to Stay in Koh Tao

Phandara Luxury Pool Villas

Wake up in your luxury villa and walk straight from your bed into your private pool overlooking the ocean at this luxury boutique hotel. This is the villa you come to to get away from the traveler crowd. Phrandara is off the beaten path and not the easiest to access. To get into town, you'll need to take the shuttle provided; don't try and ride a scooter up these steep hills. For this reason, my advice is to stay a few nights at Phandara with the intention of enjoying the villa and going on an inner journey with a book, a journal and some sun tanning!

★ **Style:** Privates Pool Villas
💸 **Budget:** $$$$
📍 **Where:** The Hills Above Sairee Beach

BOOK HERE

The Dearly Koh Tao Hostel

The Dearly is the most perfect hostel on Koh Tao that it is the only one I'm going to write about. The Dearly offers you the chance to see the island, relax solo and also make new friends to explore with. The Dearly offers free shuttles to the beach and offers free activities that make it really easy for you to connect with other travelers. The hostel has a pool, a common room, a rooftop terrace, a bar and a restaurant with free breakfast. Bonus: This hostel is extremely clean, SHA-Certified and run by local Thais! The #TravelKarma is good here.

PRO TIP: Treat yourself to a private room and you'll feel like you're staying at a social boutique resort rather than a hostel.

★ **Style:** Dorms and Privates
💸 **Budget:** $
📍 **Where:** Island central, Chalok

BOOK HERE

Blue Tao Beach Hotel

Get the beachfront room! This room has a hammock balcony where you can literally climb down off of it onto the beach and run into the ocean. This little net hammock is the best place to watch the sunset with a beer in your hand! The staff are lovely and the rooms are pristinely clean, which is totally aligned with their SHA Plus Certification! Go go go.

★ *Style:* Privates
💸 *Budget:* $$$
📍 *Where:* Sairee Beachfront

BOOK HERE

•••

Tanote Villa Hill

Tucked between jungle and palm trees overlooking the ocean, Tanote Villa Hill is breathtaking! Every single room has its own private balcony, and when you're located along a private beach, there is no bad view. The pools (yes, plural) mean that you never have to bump elbows with other vacationers or fight for a poolside lounge chair. After a full day of sunbathing, cool off at the bar or dig into a traditional Thai meal at the onsite restaurant. Then walk down to the beach and go snorkeling!

★ *Style:* Privates
💸 *Budget:* $$$
📍 *Where:* Tanote Bay

BOOK HERE

•••

Ecotao Resort

If you're a laid-back chick who loves the idea of falling asleep in a rustic little shack bungalow surrounded by palm trees with ocean views, then you'll love this place. Not to mention, they've got a big blue pool to offer you a little bit of that resort feel. Ecotao is off the beaten path but they offer a 300 baht taxi service into town whenever you need. This is the perfect escape when you want to be treated like a princess but an unplugged, off-the-grid princess.

★ *Style:* Privates
💸 *Budget:* $$$
📍 *Where:* In the Jungle of Lang Khai Bay

BOOK HERE

Koh Tao Cabana

You're going to be exhausted after your intensive dive course. The best plan is to just collapse into nature where you can recuperate in your hammock. This fabulous resort is the perfect tropical island getaway with bamboo wood and relaxed music, located near Sairee Beach.

★ *Style:* Privates
💵 *Budget:* $$
📍 *Where:* Walking Distance to Sairee Beach

BOOK HERE

. . . .

In Touch Resort

Location location location! Grand Beach Resort is smack dab in the middle of all the action located on Sairee Beach next to the best bars, shops, and restaurants, just a few steps from the ocean. The rooms are simple which keeps the price simple! The on-site restaurant lights up at night with twinkly lights everywhere, making for the perfect spot to have a drink solo (and likely end up making new friends).

★ *Style:* Private Bungalows
💵 *Budget:* $$
📍 *Where:* Sairee Beach

BOOK HERE

. . . .

View Point Resort - SHA Plus

More luxury pool villas but at a little cheaper cost! View Point Resort is a new resort with stunning ocean views! If you're not in the market to splurge on a private pool villa, you can semi-splurge on a private room with incredible ocean views instead. Similar to Phandara Luxury Villas above, View Point Resort is not easy to access, so come with the intention of chilling out with sounds of the ocean in the background.

★ *Style:* Privates Pool Villas and Ocean View Villas
💵 *Budget:* $$$
📍 *Where:* Chalok Bay

Things to Do in Koh Tao

Go Scuba Diving

Koh Tao is one of the cheapest places in the world to get your Scuba certifications

This well-preserved island is a mecca for Scuba Divers—both brand new and experienced. Divers come from all over the world to swim with whale sharks, sea turtles, eels, and National Geographic-style schools of fish. You've got lots of options when it comes to dive shops—compare prices!

I got my certification with Phoenix Divers, who took me through a 4 day Dive Course with classroom training, pool practice, and the real deal—underwater dives. Another popular dive school is Big Blue Dive School

Want to just TRY scuba diving for a day?

Here is a 1-day scuba adventure, no experience necessary: Now you can say you've been scuba diving in Thailand!

Go Snorkeling

Koh Tao has some of the best snorkeling! I won't bore you with filler here, I'll just tell you the best snorkel spots to go after when you're choosing a boat trip.

* Shark Bay
* Hin Wong Bay
* Mango Bay
* Aow Leuk

If you want to jump aboard a big ass boat and explore the underwater world of Koh Tao, this is the tour I recommend ☞

John Suwan View Point

John Suwan Viewpoint is located on the southern tip of Koh Tao, with stunning panoramic views of Chalok Baan Kao Bay, Shark Bay, and Thian Og Bay. It's a sea of crystal clear waters, green hills and palm trees!

📷 BOOKING.COM

From the base of the viewpoint, it's just a 15 minute hike to reach the top—with a 50 Baht entrance fee. Alternatively, you can hike up the 500meter hill, accessible via Freedom Beach. Also, a 50 Baht entrance fee. Neither hikes are too strenuous, but you will need to wear a pair of tennies.

💵 **Budget:** 50 Baht

🕐 **Best Time to Visit:** Between 6am for amazing sunrise views and less tourists.

🕐 **Time Needed:** Around one hour.

Visit Koh Nangyuan Island

Hop in a longtail boat on the west side of Koh Toa where you'll take a blissful 10 minute boat ride to the gorgeous shores of Koh Nangyuan. This beautifully peculiar strip of white sand beach connects three islands where you can climb, swim, and tan. Make sure to bring a camera—totally Instagram worthy. You can hire boats straight from the beach or have your hotel arrange a tour for you

Ps. They close at 5pm.

Take a Cooking Class

...with the sweetest woman, named Prawan. Not only will Prawan teach you how to cook like a local, but she'll also send you home with the recipes so that you can cook Thai food in your own kitchen for your friends and fam. This is the best souvenir to take home! Pro Tip: Ask to make Mango Sticky Rice. This is such an easy one to make at home during mango season!

Budget: $46 USD / 1,500 THB   *Book here:*

Hey...

Trust that the tours in this book are worth your time - and are also a great way to meet other travelers.

I used to be an official Tour Hater!

I would avoid tours in Thailand like the plague because I wanted to be a "real" traveler. But what really ended up happening, is that I would miss out on some of the best experiences and actually get stuck doing the touristy things I was trying to escape! Know that I hate touristy shit.

So now, I am a reformed "anti-tour" traveler who knows how to spot and avoid the touristy stuff, and steer you towards the best experiences.

Have a favorite tour you think I should recommend? Send me a link at **hello@thesologirlstravelguide.com** or tag me in your tour photos on Instagram **@SoloGirlsTravelGuide**

The more you share with me, the better experiences I can share with other solo travel girls ♥

Where to Eat in Koh Tao

Seafood By Pawn

When you've got a Thai grandmother in the kitchen, you know that this Thai food is the real deal! Seafood by Pawn has got all the classics like whole grilled fish, som tam salad, and every curry dish under the sun. They also serve Beer Lao here—definitely a must if you're a beer drinker.

♥ Where: Mae Haad Village

VegetaBowl

After a week of stir-fried Thai food, your body will start to crave clean ingredients. VegetaBowl is fresh fresh fresh with salads, smoothies, and grilled veggies to replenish all the healthy nutrients your system craves. You can go full on vegan, vegetarian and dairy-free with every type of cuisine from Mediterranean with hummus or Japanese with handrolls! Pair with a fresh coconut and your body will thank you.

♥ Where: Sairee, Near Ban's Diving
f Facebook: Vegetabowl

Thaita Italian Restaurant

Take advantage of the abundance of fresh seafood with some killer ceviche at Thaita Italian Restaurant! Of course, you can find all of the Italian classics—handmade by Italians, might I add—such as gnocchi, Bolognese, and tiramisu. Every bite is next level!

♥ Where: Sairee Beach, Next to Suksamarin Villas
f Facebook: ThaitaItalian

Barracuda Restaurant & Bar

Another popular seafood spot. Barracuda is where you can eat family style with massive platters full of shrimp, mussels, calamari, and fish that have been seasoned to perfection and served with homemade sauces that are to die for. So fresh. So worth it.

📍 **Where:** Sairee Beach
🏛 **Address:** 9/9 Moo 1
🌐 **Website:** barracudakohtao.com

Café Culture

Get your caffeine fix with some legit coffee, handcrafted in every form - and one of the best Matcha Green Tea Lattes around. This quaint little cafe sits with a beach front view making it the perfect place to wake up with a hearty Eggs Benedict or a full-on English Breakfast. Or if you're feeling really indulgent, the Banana Pancake with Nutella is to die for.

📍 **Where:** Sairee Beach
f **Facebook:** Cafe Culture Koh Tao

Tree House Cafe

Incredible views. Garden-grown food. Run by Thai owners who pour their heart and soul into everything from the plate to the hospitality. Tree House Cafe is definitely worth your time whether for lunch or dinner (at sunset). Order the Spicy Glass Noodle Salad with Prawns...and try to order in Thai: "Yam Woon sen Gung".

📍 **Where:** 10-minute motorbike drive from Mae Haad Pier
🌐 **Website:** https://treehousecafe.business.site/

Chill Beach Bar And Grill Koh Tao

When you are hungry but also want to possibly meet some new people or pick up a hot guy who is also traveling solo...this is the beachfront spot you want. It's just a little beachfront bar with mats in the sand and little tables on the ground where you eat fresh seafood with a sunset view. Order a whole coconuts or cold beer and watch the sun go down and the party life start to pop up. Get a little tipsy and dip your toes in the ocean after your meal.

Hippo Burger

One of the best burgers in Thailand is randomly on this little island in the middle of the ocean. Here's the deal: After you've been in the water all day long, you're going to be starving and sometimes you just want food you don't have to think about. If you've had enough curry by now, sink your teeth into a juicy Hippo burger...and hey, they have veggie burgers, too, if that's your thing.

♀ Where: Sairee Beach Sairee Beach
f Facebook: Hippo Burger Koh Tao

Lung Pae

Looking for a quaint candle-lit dinner to give you a reason to dress up? Well, you can always dress up (you're on vacation on an island) but Lung Pae's charming setting really calls for a cute outfit. Perched on the hillside with a view, their pan-Asian menu offers mouthwatering dishes. And hey, if you want to get tipsy, Lung Pae provides shuttle service from your hotel or the pier. Message them to arrange ahead of time. Ps. This place isn't expensive.

♀ Where: Sairee Beach Sairee Beach 10-minute motorbike drive from Mae Haad Pier, near Treehouse Cafe
f Facebook: Lung Pae Restuarant

Whitening

The date night spot and/or the celebration spot. I know the name is weird, but this place is elegant. Think wine, oysters, "catch of the day" - the whole sexy shebang! It's also beachfront. I will mention however, this isn't the cheapest Thai food, but the ambiance is worth it! Expect to pay around 190 thb/$6 usd for a curry (hey, that's expensive in Thailand).

♀ Where: Sairee Beach
f Facebook: Whitening Koh Tao

Breeze Koh Tao

Sharing food? Come to Breeze Koh Tao where your posse can share cheese plates, mezze platters and even dessert boards! Breeze is known for their sandwiches, steaks and western foods from home - but really is my pick for a place to do appetizers or desserts with an ocean view. Located near Mae Haad Pier, this is a great place to grab a bite before or after your ferry!

♀ Where: Mae Haad Pier
⊕ Website: Breezekohtao.com

WANT MORE ISLANDS?

Want to get off the beaten path to quieter beaches?

You need the Thailand Islands and Beaches book!

This Thailand Guide: The highlights

The Islands and Beaches Guide: The roads less traveled

Get it on Amazon

Search *"Alexa West Islands"* or follow this QR code to book

Nightlife in Koh Tao

✋**Be Aware:** Sairee Beach has a sinister reputation.

☞ **Full Disclosure:** There have been 11 murders and a handful of rapes in the past several years on the island. The most recent incident of drug and rape happening to a British girl in August 2018. These all happened in the party area of the island.

This behavior is extremely rare for Thailand, but an increasing pattern on Sairee Beach, particularly at Leo Bar.

I love Koh Tao for its beaches and diving. I recommend that when you go to Koh Tao, don't even plan on partying. But if you do...here are some rules to follow.

Rule #1: No Bucket Drinks. Beers only.

Rule #2: Do not let your drink out of your sight!

Rule #3: Do not let a man buy you a drink.

Rule #4: Never ever walk on the beach past midnight, not even with a tall strong man who you think can protect you.

Rule #5: Be home by midnight.

Now that you're terrified (sorry bout that, babe), here's what you can do.

✓ Have some cocktails on the beach during the day and around dinner time.

✓ Watch the fire spinners on the beach and hang out with a big group of travelers

✓ Drink some beers and head back to your hotel by midnight

The predators on the island are Thai men looking for that solo backpacker girl who is in party mode and can be easily drugged.

Also, the police aren't much help if something does go wrong, either.

If you do want to go out, check out these places that with safe reputations.

Good Vibe Bar

After a day of scuba diving and snorkeling, kicking your feet up with a really yummy cocktail and live music is the perfect way to end the day. Good Vibe Bar is more intimate than the raging beach parties, and you'll have a better chance of meeting some strangers and striking up a conversation, rather than getting wasted.

♀ Where: Maehaad

CoCo Bar

Sairee Beach's go-to party spot, CoCo Bar is a must-visit. This place is like a magnet for social creatures. Show up alone and you'll make friends within no time. Amazing cocktails and music that you actually want to listen to. Plus… there's always lots of cute boys here.

♀ Where: Sairee Beach

Lotus Beach Bar

Grab a seat near the water's edge. Lotus has comfy floor tables and bean bags where you can sip cocktails with your toes in the sand while you watch Thai fire spinners perform some questionable, yet entertaining, stunts. Come for sunset and don't be surprised if you spend your whole night here.

♀ Where: Sairee Beach

Avoid Fish Bowl Bar and Leo Bar

Yes, it's the most popular party spot on the island…but this is where the majority of crime takes place. Don't let other travelers hype you up that this is a good idea, either. It's so easy to get swept up in the mood but you can find an even better mood elsewhere on the island. I pinkie promise.

Getting Around Koh Tao

Motorbike

By now, you know that I don't recommend using a motorbike on Koh Tao or Koh Phangan. This is also not the place to learn how to drive a scooter with an island consisting of steep and risky hills. If you rent a bike here, use extreme caution. Rental shops require you to leave a passport or a very high deposit – because crashes are so common. Rentals start at 200 THB to 300.

Walk

The island is relatively small so almost everything worth visiting is within walking distance, via Koh Tao's cobblestone roads.

Taxi

Not really taxis, but pick-up trucks, rather. The trucks transfer you from piers to hotels and can also be hired to take you to viewpoints or other beaches on the island. However, they are expensive at 300 baht for a quick ride.

ITINERARIES FOR
Thailand

———

The biggest mistake I see girls making when planning
a trip to Thailand is trying to see it ALL!

Thailand is huge. While trying to cover so many places
and visit so many beaches in such short amounts of time,
you end up rushing the most beautiful experiences.

Everyone you talk to about Thailand is going to have an opinion
of where you HAVE to go and what you HAVE to see.
Yeah yeah yeah, we get it.

Everyone cherishes their experiences,
and naturally wants to share them with you.
But then you just get overloaded with this massive checklist
and now your vacation is a chore.

In order for you to have the best possible experience,
you've got to be realistic with your time.

Here are some realistic itineraries to help you plan an unforgettable trip with
just the right amount of activity to relaxation.

Want me to plan your trip for you?

I make Bucket List Vacations come true.
Visit the Trip Planning section on TheSoloGirlsTravelGuide.com

2-WEEK: BANGKOK, BEACHES, JUNGLE & ELEPHANTS

Day 1: Bangkok
❋**A.M.**

→ Fly into Bangkok & stay in the Khao San Road Area

→ Follow my 1-Day Bangkok Itineraries for 2.5 days

Day 2: Bangkok
❋**A.M.**

→ Relax at your hotel pool or bar

✴**P.M.**

→ Spend the evening in Chinatown

Day 3: Khao Sok
❋**A.M.**

→ Wake up early for a floating market tour with Pook or another similar tour I've provided for you

→ Before you go, check out of your hotel and leave your bags at the hotel reception - you'll return after checkout time but won't be sleeping here tonight.

✴**P.M.**

→ Take the sleeper train from Bangkok's Chinatown to Surat Thani (leaving in Bangkok the evening and arriving in the morning)

→ Travel to your Khao Sok hotel

→ Join in on the Night Safari

Day 4: Overnight at Cheow Lan Lake

→ Floating bungalows and kayaking on the lake

Day 5: Tour Day in Khao Sok
❋**A.M.**

→ Morning boat Safari

→ Head back to Khao Sok

✴**P.M.**

→ Float down the river and explore the town

Day 6: Car to Krabi + Boat to Railay

*A.M.
→ Leave around 11am, get into Krabi around 2pm
→ Head to Railay via long tail boat
*P.M.
→ Take your shoes off and and go check in to your hotel
→ Have lunch at Railay Family Restaurant
→ Party on Railay East
→ Get drunk food at Last Bar

Day 7: Railay
*A.M.
→ Spend the morning at Phra Nang Cave Beach
*P.M.
→ At 1pm, go on a snorkel adventure with Krabi Sunset Cruise

Day 8: Boat to Koh Phi Phi

(Alternative, skip Phi Phi and fly to Koh Samui instead. Koh Samui is a more sophisticated island with less boat trip - from Samui, fly to Chiang Mai afterwards).

*A.M.
→ Shop, eat and party - watch the fire show on the beach
→ Arrange your boat tour for the next morning

Day 9: Boat Tour
*A.M.
→ Visit Maya Bay, Monkey Island and the Blue Lagoon
→ Eat and enjoy your last day on Koh Phi Phi
*P.M.
→ Go watch the fire shows on the beach

Day 10: Head Back to Krabi Town or Phuket > Chiang Mai
*A.M.
→ Catch a boat back to Krabi or Phuket and head to the airport from the pier
→ Fly to Chiang Mai (there are flights leaving all day)

→ Check into your Chiang Mai Hotel

→ Throw your bags down and head to the night market

Day 11: Chiang Mai
☀A.M.

→ In the morning, go to Elephant Nature Park or a similar ethical elephant sanctuary

★P.M.

→ Come back and get a massage at the Women's Prison

→ Go to North Gate Night Market and hit the jazz bar across the street afterwards

Day 12: Chiang Mai
☀A.M.

→ Temple hopping day - visit Doi Kham and Doi Suthep

★P.M.

→ Take a cooking class in the afternoon

Day 13: Chiang Mai
☀A.M.

→ Zipline with The Gibbon Experience

★P.M.

→ Go to The Chiang Mai Cabaret Show or watch a Muay Thai Fight at night.

Day 14: Head Back Home
→ Your connecting flight will likely be in Bangkok

Day 1: Bangkok

✱ P.M.

→ Fly into Bangkok & stay in the Khao San Road Area

→ Go straight to I love Thai Food and order the Khao Soi

→ Explore Khao San Road with food, drinks, shopping, and live music

→ Get a foot massage on Rambuttri Road amongst the chaos

Day 2: Chiang Mai

☀ A.M.

→ Wake up early for a floating market tour with Pook or explore the temples via Tuk Tuk

→ Before you go, check out of your hotel and leave your bags at the hotel reception - you'll return after checkout time but won't be sleeping here tonight.

✱ P.M.

→ Take the sleeper train from Bangkok's Chinatown to Chiang Mai

Day 3: Chiang Mai

☀ A.M.

→ Arrive around 8am

→ Put your bags down at your hotel - you likely won't be able to check in yet

✱ P.M.

→ Go to 7-Eleven and eat a toastie

→ Explore the Old City by foot

→ Get a massage or take a cooking class

→ Come back to check-in, shower and rest or hit the pool

→ Visit a Night Market or the Night Bazaar for dinner & people watching

Day 4: Chiang Mai

☀ **A.M.**

→ Wake up early for a day spent at an elephant sanctuary (or consider spending the night there!)

✳ **P.M.**

→ For dinner, visit Chiang Mai's best Thai restaurant, Lert Ros, for grilled seafood and Mango Sticky Rice for dessert

Day 5: Chiang Mai > Krabi or Koh Samui

☀ **A.M.**

→ Up early to hike Doi Kham or Doi Su Thep

✳ **P.M.**

→ Take a flight to Krabi or Koh Samui in the afternoon

Day 6-10: Live the Beach Life

Follow my itineraries above

📷 @MEAGANSTANS

8-DAYS: ISLAND HOPPING & ELEPHANTS

Day 1: Koh Samui

→ Fly into Bangkok or Phuket - and get a connecting flight directly to Koh Samui

→ Spend 2 days on Samui

→ Make sure to visit the Elephant Jungle Sanctuary

Day 3: Koh Phangan

→ Spend 2 days on Koh Phangan

Day 5: Koh Tao

→ Spend 3 days on Koh Tao

Day 8: Fly Out

→ The last day, get a boat to Koh Samui and fly out

→ Make sure you give yourself plenty of time to get between islands. If you have an early flight, spend the night on Koh Samui the night before your flight

WANT A CUSTOMIZED ITINERARY?

I create dream vacations based on your Travel Bucket List!

Find out more at TheSoloGirl'sTravelGuide.com/Trip-Plans or message me directly at hello@thesologirlstravelguide.com

ITINERARIES FOR THAILAND

Thai Festivals & Holidays

January 22nd, 2023 / Chinese New Year

Celebrate the Chinese New Year in Chinatown—of course! Yarowat in Bangkok will have celebrations and parades in the streets, as well as food and festivities within temple grounds.

March 6th, 2023 / Makha Bucha (Magha Puja)

Marking Buddha's enlightenment, this is a very special holiday around South East Asia. Thai monks and locals will visit temples to give offerings, pray, and chant. You are welcome to visit any temple and join in. PS: Bars will not be open on this day.

Most Popular Celebration Spots:
★ Wat Saket Bangkok/Golden Mountain, Bangkok
★ Wat Benjamabopit/The Marble Temple, Bangkok

April 13th—April 15th / Songkran (Thai New Year)

Thailand's water festival is one of the biggest holidays of the year for both Thais and tourists. The water fight madness represents cleansing for the New Year in hopes for a bountiful harvest. The most popular location for Songkran is Chiang Mai, where for 4 days—you can't leave your hotel without getting soaked by water guns or strangers dumping water over your head. It's wild.

Most Popular Celebration Spots:
★ Central Chiang Mai
★ Bangkok's Silom Area
★ Chaweng Beach, Koh Samui

July 14ᵗʰ, 2022 / Beginning of Buddhist Lent

Although Buddhist lent lasts into October, you will find many celebrations around Bangkok that celebrate Buddhist culture. At major temples around Thailand, you can witness candle making, flower ceremonies, and parades—all of which welcome tourists to participate. PS: Bars will be closed so you might as well join in.

Most Popular Celebration Spots (check for specific dates):
★ Lad Cha Do Market, Ayutthaya
★ Most Thai Temples, Bangkok

October 13ᵗʰ / Passing of King Bhumibol

Thailand lost their beloved King Bhumibol in 2016. He was loved and respected deeply. On October 13ᵗʰ, Thai People will wear black in commemoration and there will be a moment silence held across the country at 3.52pm. It's not always for sure, but there's a strong chance that alcohol will not be sold on this day.

Most Popular Celebration Spots:
★ The Grand Palace, Bangkok

November 9ᵗʰ, 2022 / The Lantern Festival

Loi Krathong is a once in a lifetime festival where thousands of lanterns are released into the sky. This Buddhist holiday represents the birth, enlightenment, and death of Buddha—and is celebrated nationwide.

Most Popular Celebration Spots:
★ Ping River or Nawarat bridge, Chiang Mai
★ Bejakitti Park, Bangkok

You can find many places around Thailand to release water lanterns, but if you want the glittering sky lanterns, you should be in Chiang Mai! Book your hotels in advance!

December 31ˢᵗ – January 1ˢᵗ / Western New Year

You can find fabulous parties in any major city or beach town in Thailand! Expect glittery dresses and drink specials just like back home.

THINGS TO KNOW

How to Go to Other Destinations in Thailand

Advice: Use 12go.asia for everything ☞

PRO TIP: There are 2 airports in Bangkok- Suvarnabhumi Airport (BKK/ SVB) and Don Mueang Airport (DMK). Both have international and domestic flights! Check your ticket!

CHIANG MAI

Chiang Mai has mountains, elephants, and laid back vibes and serves as digital nomad central! You can also use Chiang Mai as a jumping off point to Pai or Mae Hong Son.

By Sleeper Train

A must-have experience if you've got time! The Sleeper Train is comfortable, affordable, and saves you one night's accommodation. Buy your tickets at least 3 days in advance! You can do this via a travel agency or by going directly to the station.

📍 **Point of Departure:** Hua Lamphong Station
★ **Best Times:** 6:10pm and 7:30pm
⊙ **Duration:** 13-14 hours (of sleep time, reading time, and seeing the countryside time)

TRAIN PRO TIPS...

✳ Go with the 2nd class fan option. 1st class is just the same but blasts the air conditioning so high that it's a miserably cold ride.

✳ Try to get a bottom bunk! They are more comfortable and you don't have to climb a ladder to go to the bathroom in the middle of the night!

✻ If you're visiting during Thai holidays, buy your train tickets as early as you can. You can book 1 month in advance!

By Plane
◉ Point of Departure: BKK/SVB or DMK
◉ Duration: 1 hour & 10 minutes
◉ Budget: Starting at $60 USD / 2,000 baht

By Bus
◉ Point of Departure: Mo Chit Bus Terminal (Northern Bus Terminal)
◉ When: Every hour between 5:30am and 10pm
◉ Duration: Roughly 10 hours
◉ Budget: Starting at $16 USD / 530 baht

• •

KHAO SOK

Home to Khao Sok National Park and Cheow Lan Lake - this is super off the beaten path but fun to get to!

From Bangkok...
○ *Option 1:* Take the sleeper train from Bangkok to Surat Thani Town.
☞ **Book:** Train #167 with Thai Railways in 2nd Class Sleeper AC
◉ Departs Bangkok: 6:30pm
◉ Arrives in Surat Thani: 7:48am
❤ **Ticket:** Get your ticket on 12go.asia - book the bottom bunk if possible.
➡ **Next:** From the train station, get a bus or a private taxi to Surat Thani.

○ *Option 2:* Fly to Surat Thani Airport
➡ **Next:** From the train station, get a bus or a private taxi to Surat Thani.

From Krabi...
Take a Public Bus or Shared Van

◉ Duration: 5 hours   **◉ Duration:** 2.5 hours
◉ Budget: $7-$11 USD   **◉ Budget:** About $75

KRABI

Krabi is a dream come true with a selection of gorgeous beaches such as Railay or Tonsai, access to day trip islands, and nearby to the popular Koh Phi Phi.

By Plane
♀ Point of Departure: BKK/SVB airport or DMK airport
☉ When: All day every day
☉ Duration: 1 hour & 20 mins
🖙 Budget: Starting at $60 USD / 2,000 baht

By Bus
♀ Point of Departure: Bangkok's Southern Bus Terminal or Khao San Road
☉ When: Typically, overnight busses leaving in the evenings
☉ Duration: 10-13 hours
🖙 Budget: Starting at $30 USD / 1,000 baht

AYUTTHAYA

Thailand's ancient capital city founded around 1350, Ayutthaya's sprawling historical grounds are scattered with sacred temples, ancient relics, and fascinating architecture.

By Minivan
♀ Point of Departure: Mo Chit Bus Terminal (Northern Bus Terminal) & Khao San Road
☉ When: Buses depart every 30 minutes from 6am-6pm
☉ Duration: 1.5 hours
🖙 Budget: Starting at $3 USD / 100 baht

By Bus
♀ Point of Departure: Bangkok's Southern Bus Terminal & Khao San Road
☉ When: Every 20 minutes from 4:30am-6pm
☉ Duration: 2 hours
🖙 Budget: Starting at $3 USD / 100 baht

By Train

♥ Point of Departure: Hua Lamphong Train Station
☉ When: 32 trains per day from 4:20am – 10:45pm
☉ Duration: 2-2.5 hours depending on the train you choose
Budget: Starting at $0.60 USD / 20 baht

SURAT THANI & THE ISLANDS

To get to Koh Tao, Koh Phangan, and Koh Samui from Bangkok – you've got options, girl! You can travel via Boat, Train, Bus or Plane. The main transport hub is the mainland town of Surat Thani. They've been handling tourism so long that if you just get dropped off in town, someone will be ready to get you where ya' need to go.

Every transport company and every pier offers transport to all 3 islands – so the following rules apply to all 3 islands.

Bus to Surat Thani Town

If you're on a tight budget, you can bus/minivan down to Surat Thani Town and then transport yourself to the pier. This can save you around $10-$15.
♥ Point of Departure: Southern Bus Terminal- also known as Sai Tai Mai
☉ When: 2 buses at 7am & 6 buses between 6:30pm-11pm
☉ Duration: 12 hours
Budget: Starting at $15 USD / 500 baht

Minivan

♥ Point of Departure: Khao San Road
☉ When: Mornings and evenings- check with a local travel agency
☉ Duration: 10 hours
Budget: Starting at $25 USD / 800 baht

Bus + Ferry Combo via Chumphon

To have everything organized for you, get a combo ticket from Bangkok!
♥ Point of Departure: Khao San Road or Hua Lamphong Train Station
☉ When: Most buses leave Bangkok around 6 or 7pm
☉ Duration: 8 hours + 5 hours.
Budget: $36 USD / 1200 baht

PRO TIPS: You will find plenty of tour companies and hostels selling an island transportation package on Khao San Road. If you're in the Sukhumvit Area, go to Bodega Hostel where they sell the combo for cheap – you can buy it the day before you go!

A long bus might sound like a nightmare…but it's the best way to meet other travelers on the way to the islands.

By Plane + Ferry Combo Via Surat Thani

📍 *Point of Departure:* BKK/SVB Airport or DMK Airport
🕐 *When:* All day every day
🕐 *Duration:* 1 hour & 10 minutes
🎟️ *Budget:* Starting at $30 USD / 1,000 baht

You'll fly to Surat Thani town. At the airport, there will be a tour desk offering tickets for the shuttle bus + ferry boat to the islands.

Ferry operations are all throughout the day from 9am-5:30pm. The price of the ferry starts at 600 baht, depending on the company and your destination

By Train

You can get a daytime train or the overnight sleeper train- depending on when you're catching the ferry.

📍 *Point of Departure:* Hua Lamphong Railway Station
🕐 *When:* There's one train at 8am, and 14 trains from 13:00-19:30
🕐 *Duration:* 9-12 hours
🎟️ *Budget:* Starting at $25 USD / 850 baht

From Koh Phangan or Koh Samui

Easily hop on a ferry boat or a speed boat to Koh Phangan from one of the other islands – as short as 1.5 hours.

MINI
Directory
FOR THAILAND

IMPORTANT STUFF

Tourist Police – English Speaking

📱 **Phone:** 1155 (free call from any phone) or 678-6800

🏢 **Address:** TPI Tower, 25/26 Liab Khong Rd, Chong Nonsi Junction, New Chan Rd

Samitivej Sukhumvit Hospital

📍 **Where:** Sukhumvit BTS Phrom Phong

🏢 **Address:** 133 Sukhumvit 49

🕐 **Open:** 24 hours

EMBASSIES

British Embassy

📱 **Emergency Line:** 02 305 8333

🏢 **Address:** 14 Wireless Rd Lumpini Pathumwan

American Embassy

📱 **Emergency Line:** 02-205-4000

🏢 **Address:** 95 Wireless Rd Khwaeng Lumphini Pathumwan

Canadian Embassy

📱 **Emergency Line:** 02646-4300

🏢 **Address:** 15th Floor, Abdulrahim Place 990 Rama IV Rd Bangrak

Australian Embassy

📱 **Emergency Line:** 02 344 6300

🏢 **Address:** 37 South Sathorn Rd Tungmahamek, Sathorn

GYNECOLOGY SERVICES & FEMALE STUFF

Women's Center (OB/GYN) – Vejthani Hospital Bangkok

All of the services including birth control, ultrasounds, STD testing, etc.

🕐 **Open:** 24 hours

↻ **How to Get There:** When you make an appointment, the hospital will send a shuttle bus to pick you up. Or you can take a taxi from On Nut Thong Lor

🏛 **Address:** 1 Soi Lat Phrao 111

Birth Control

You can buy birth control pills and contraception over the counter in Thailand

📍 **Where:** All pharmacies and Boots Drug Stores

Morning After Pill

📍 **Where:** Every pharmacy carries it under "Postinor" or "Madona" (I know, right?) for 40–60 Baht

Unwanted Pregnancy –Klong Tun Medical Center

🕐 **Open:** 24/7

↻ **How to Get There:** BTS Phra Khanong, Next to Cabbages and Condoms Restaurant on Sukhumvit 12

🏛 **Address:** 3284 New Petchburi Rd Bangkapi Khet Huai Khwang

📱 **Phone:** 02 319 2101

For more information, check out gynopedia.org/Bangkok

And please, just visit WorldNomads. com to check out Travel Insurance. It's better to have it and not need it; than to need it and not have it.

Coming to Thailand and have questions, want some tips or just want to chat about life in Asia?
Reach out to me on Instagram @SoloGirlsTravelGuide

No seriously.
I'd love to hear from you and stalk your trip. ♥

THE TRUE STORY OF HOW THE
Solo Girl's Travel Guide
WAS BORN

I was robbed in Cambodia.

Sure, the robber was a child and yes, I might have drunkenly put my purse down in the sand while flirting with an irresistible Swedish boy...but that doesn't change the fact that I found myself without cash, a debit card and hotel key at 1am in a foreign country.

My mini robbery, however, doesn't even begin to compare to my other travel misadventures. I've also been scammed to tears by taxi drivers, idiotically taken ecstasy in a country with the death penalty for drugs and missed my flight because how was I supposed to know that there are two international airports in Bangkok?

It's not that I'm a total idiot.

It's just that...people aren't born savvy travelers.

I'm not talking about hedonistic vacationers who spend their weekend at a resort sipping Mai Tais. I'm talking about train-taking, market-shopping, street food-eating travelers!

Traveling is not second (or third or fourth) nature; it's a skill that only comes with sweaty on-the-ground experience...especially for women!

In the beginning of my travels (aka the first 5 years), I made oodles of travel mistakes. And thank god I did. These mistakes eventually turned me into the resourceful, respected and established travel guru that I am today.

A travel guru that was spawned through a series of being lost, hospitalized,

Year-after-year and country-after-country, I started learning things like…

✔ Always check your hostel mattress for bed bugs.

✔ Local alcohol is usually toxic and will give you a hangover that lasts for days.

✔ The world isn't "touristy" once you stop traveling like a tourist.

✔ And most importantly, the best noodle shops are always hidden in back alleys.

After nearly 11 years of traveling solo around the world (4 continents and 26 countries, but who's counting?) – I travel like a gosh darn pro. I save money, sleep better, haggle harder, fly fancier, and speak foreign languages that help me almost almost blend in with the locals despite my blonde hair.

Yeah yeah yeah. I guess it's cool being a travel icon. But shoot…

Do you know how much money, how many panic attacks, and how many life-threatening risks I could have saved and/or avoided if only someone had freakin' queued me into all of this precious information along the way? A lot. A lotta' lot.

So, why didn't I just pick up a travel guide and start educating myself like an adult? I had options…right? I could've bought a copy of Lonely Planet…but how the hell am I supposed to smuggle a 5-pound brick in my carry-on bag? Or DK Eyewitness, perhaps? Hell no. I don't have 8 hours to sift through an encyclopedia and decode details relevant to my solo adventure.

There was no travel guide that would have spared my tears or showed me how to travel safer and smarter.

The book I needed didn't exist. So, I freakin' wrote it myself.

What travel guide do you need me to write next?

Tell me on Instagram ♥ @SoloGirlsTravelGuide

THE 11 TRAVEL COMMANDMENTS
OF Solo Girl's Travel Guide

01 Be an Explorer, Not a Tourist.

Some people travel just for the photo. While others travel to find the unfamiliar, connect with strangers, expand their minds, and try new things for the sake of trying new things. Which kind of traveler are you?

02 Leave Room for Happenstance

Don't overstuff your itinerary. Slow down, be where you are and leave room for serendipity! Literally, schedule serendipity time so the universe can take the lead.

03 Vote with your Dollar

When possible, choose to support local businesses that operate ethically - aka businesses that respect the environment, benefit their local communities, don't take advantage of animals and just treat their staff really really well.

04 Look for the Gift

Love your mistakes! With every bump in the road comes a gift. Miss a bus? Look for the gift. Lose your room key? Look for the gift. Get dumped on your honeymoon? Look for the gift! There will always be a gift.

05 Stay Curious

Ask questions! Ask questions when you like something and ask questions when you don't understand something. Out loud or in your head. And whenever you feel judgment arise, replace it with a question instead.

06 More Stories, Less Photos

Take a couple photos and then put your phone away. While everyone else is taking shitty sunset photos that never look as good on camera…you are really there, experiencing every shade of color in real time. Take note in your head of the story you will bring home - of the people you see, the food you smell, the monkeys in the trees! Look up, not down.

07 Count Experiences, Not Passport Stamps

You can never "do" Mexico. You can go to Mexico 50 times and still each experience will be different than the last. Travel to live, not to brag.

08 Mind your Impact

Leave every place better than you found it. Take a piece of trash from the beach and be kind to people you meet. Bring your own water bottle, canvas bag, and reusable straw to avoid single-use plastics.

09 Avoid Voluntourism

People are not zoo animals. Playing with children at orphanages, temporarily teaching English in villages or volunteering at women's shelters hurt more than they help. Want to volunteer with a positive impact? Check out my blog at TheSoloGirlsTravelGuide.com/travel-blog

10 Carry your Positivity

Ever had a crappy day and then a stranger smiles at you and flips your entire mood? Travel can be hard, but your positivity will be your secret weapon. Happy vibes are contagious. Even when we don't speak the local language, a smile or a random act of kindness tips the universal scale in the right direction for you and the people you meet along your journey.

11 Trust your Gut

Listen to that little voice inside you. When something doesn't feel right, back away. When something feels good, lean. Your intuition will lead you to beautiful places, unforgettable moments, and new lifelong friends.

BONUS: Drink where the Locals Drink, Eat Where the Locals Eat

Even if it's under a tarp outside a mini mart. This is how you discover the best food and make the most meaningful connections.

It feeeeeeeels good to travel good.

A CONFESSION:

I bend the rules. Sometimes I stay in an all-inclusive resort instead of a locally owned guesthouse. Sometimes I go to McDonalds because I want a taste of home. And sometimes, especially when I'm tired or hungry, I'm not all sunshine and rainbows to be around.

But my moral travel compass does not bend for things that matter to me. I'll never leave a piece of trash on the beach. I'll never support elephant riding. I'd rather stay home than go on a Carnival Cruise even if it was free. Decide what matters to you now, let that guide you as you travel but let yourself be human.

Comfort yourself when you need comforting and eat the forbidden fruit sparingly. When you do make mistakes, brush yourself off and do better next time. No one's path is perfect but I'm proud of you for making your path better.

THIS TRIP.

**THIS IS WHEN YOU DISCOVER
EXACTLY WHO YOU ARE.**

TRUST YOURSELF.

WANT THE BEST TRIP EVER?

**Let's check or create your itinerary.
And answer any other questions you might have.**

Book your 20-minute call here.

calendly.com/alexawest/travelchats

Or scan here to schedule your call...

DID YOU LEAVE
A REVIEW?

**As a self-published author –
doing this whole publishing thing by myself –
reviews are what keeps
The Solo Girl's Travel Guide growing.**

If you found my guidebook to be helpful,
please leave me a review on Amazon.com

Your review helps other girls find this book
and experience a truly life-changing trip.

Ps. I read every single review.
Leave me a review here — it will just take a sec!

PASS IT ON!

This guide book is meant to change lives.
Don't let it sit on a shelf forever and ever.

Before you give this book to a friend
who needs a travel push
or before you leave it in the hostel
for the next travel girl to find…

On the back cover...

✧ write your name,
✧ your Instagram,
✧ and the dates you traveled.

This is your legacy, too.

xoxo, Alexa

WHERE NEXT?

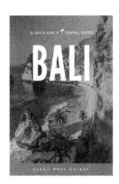

BALI

**THAILAND:
ISLANDS & BEACHES**

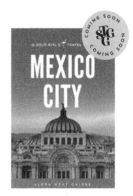

MEXICO CITY

SOUTH KOREA

JAPAN

VIETNAM

And More...
Get The Whole Collection.

Made in the USA
Las Vegas, NV
13 May 2023

72024726R00175